Glass Art

The Easy Way
to a Stained Glass Look

GLASS ART
The Easy Way
to a Stained Glass Look

Sterling Publishing Co., Inc. New York
A Sterling/Chapelle Book

Chapelle:
- Jo Packham, Owner
- Karmen Quinney, Editor
- Staff: Marie Barber, Ann Bear, Areta Bingham, Kass Burchett, Rebecca Christensen, Marilyn Goff, Shirley Heslop, Holly Hollingsworth, Sherry Hope, Shawn Hsu, Susan Jorgensen, Pauline Locke, Barbara Milburn, Linda Orton, Rhonda Rainey, Leslie Ridenour, and Cindy Stoeckl

Plaid Enterprises, Inc. Publication Staff:
- Mickey Baskett, Editor
- Sylvia Carrol, Phyllis Mueller—Copy Editors
- Laney Crisp McClure, Susan Mickey—Stylists
- Jeff Herr, Jerry Mucklow—Photography
- Dianne Miller—Graphics
- Rachel Watkins, Suzanne Yoder—Marketing

Plaid Enterprises, Inc. Design Staff:
The following artists, talented in the field of glass art, have contributed to the projects in this book:

Kim Ballor   Sue Leonard

Laura Brunson   Julie Schreiner

Jan Cumber   Carol Smith

Wendy Dyer   Renee Smith

Jacque Hennington   Kirsten Werner

Library of Congress Cataloging-in-Publication Data

Glass art: the easy way to a stained glass look / Plaid.
    p. cm.
    "A Sterling/Chapelle book."
    Includes index.
    ISBN 0-8069-8173-3
    1. Glass craft — Patterns. 2. Glass painting and staining — Patterns. I. Plaid Enterprises.
TT298.G567   1998   98-3573
748.5—dc21   CIP

10 9 8 7 6 5 4 3 2 1

Published by Sterling Publishing Company, Inc.,
387 Park Avenue South, New York, NY 10016
© 1998 by Chapelle Limited
Distributed in Canada by Sterling Publishing
% Canadian Manda Group, One Atlantic Avenue, Suite 105,
Toronto, Ontario, Canada M6K 3E7
Distributed in Great Britain and Europe by Cassell PLC,
Wellington House, 125 Strand, London WC2R 0BB,
England
Distributed in Australia by Capricorn Link (Australia) Pty
Ltd., P.O. Box 6651, Baulkham Hills, Business Centre,
NSW 2153, Australia
Printed in the United States of America
All rights reserved

Sterling ISBN 0-8069-8173-3

If you have any questions or comments or would like information on specialty products featured in this book, please contact: Chapelle Ltd., Inc., P.O. Box 9252 Ogden, UT 84409 (801) 621-2777 • FAX (801) 621-2788

Contents

Introduction

The beauty of glass art is deeper than its exquisite and professional appearance. Glass art painting is inexpensive, versatile, and easy.

Of course, the look is most important. Cut and pieced stained glass is an intricate and expensive artcraft. With glass art painting, you can create the look of authentic stained glass without the expense or skill. Windows in your home can become works of art that also filter light and provide privacy. Or, a glass art border design can be used around an unpainted area to maintain (and frame) an outdoor view. Yes, the glass art paint can be applied to these vertical surfaces right where they are. Windows of all kinds can be decorated, including windows in doors and sidelights. Other large scale projects include framed or unframed glass or plastic panels, which can be hung in windows or in front of some other light source and on large mirrors with border designs.

Glass art paint is very versatile. Three-dimensional shapes can also be decorated with this product. You can make self-adhering suncatchers for windows or patio doors and an almost unlimited array of home decor items, ranging from jars to display plates, to candleholders and much more.

Whether large or small, pick your glass art painting project and decorate your home or make outstanding gift items. Most of all, have fun!

SUPPLIES YOU WILL NEED

Translucent Textured Glass Art Paint:

Glass art paint is a special waterbase paint that dries to a transparent, textured finish, simulating the look of custom stained glass. It can be applied to glass or plastic surfaces. Available in many beautiful colors, glass art paint comes in a plastic squeeze bottle with an applicator tip, so it is easy to apply paint directly from the bottle to surfaces. All colors are available in 2 oz. bottles; Crystal Clear is also available in 8 oz. bottles.

- Do not apply glass art paint to surfaces when temperatures are lower than 45 degrees or above 90 degrees. Extremes in temperature during the application and curing process can cause cracking and distortion.

- Do not use outdoors. Do not use in environments that are not temperature-controlled, or on surfaces that are in frequent contact with water or heavy condensation.

Simulated Leading:

Simulated leading is made to look like lead strips. Simply squeeze the leading from the bottle tip to outline designs. It is available in 2 oz., 4oz., and 8 oz. squeeze bottles. Use the 8 oz. size for the larger projects.

- Simply squeeze the leading from the bottle tip to outline designs.

- Do not use outdoors. Do not use in environments that are not temperature-controlled, or on surfaces that are in frequent contact with water or heavy condensation.

Leading Blanks:

Plastic 8" x 10" leading blank sheets are used as a surface to create separate lead lines for your designs. Entire designs can also be created on these blanks, then they can be removed and applied to your windows or other surfaces.

Styrene Blanks:

Styrene blanks are used as another surface on which you can create the look of stained glass. These blanks can be painted, then framed and/or suspended.

Patterns:

Patterns are given with the projects. Some are full-size for the project as shown. Others need to be enlarged on a copy machine. The percentage of enlargement is given to attain the size of the project as shown in this book.

- Reduce or enlarge on a copy machine as needed to adjust it to the size of your individual window or decorative accessory. To figure reduction and enlargement percentages for provided patterns, use the following formulas:

  Larger Desired Size ÷ Actual Size = Enlargement %
  Example: 11" ÷ 7.5" = 1.4 (140%)

  Smaller Desired Size ÷ Actual Size = Reduction %
  Example: 4" ÷ 7.5" = .53 (53%)

  Measure for both height and width of the surface. Choose the smaller percentage to fit all within desired area.

- Trace the designs on tracing paper to keep the book intact. Place pattern behind or under glass surface or transfer to glass with black transfer paper.

Colors are indicated on the patterns by numbers. These numbers represent the colors given in the Color Key below.

- If two or more numbers are used with a + sign, mix the colors completely to create another color.

- If two or more numbers are used with a /, loosely blend or swirl the colors together within the section.

- If numbers appear within a circle(s), marbleize the colors within that section. Apply the background color, then apply dots of color indicated in the circle(s). Use the applicator tip of bottle or toothpick to swirl colors together.

- If a dotted line appears, flip the design so that it mirrors the design.

Color Key:

01 = Crystal Clear	19 = Gold Sparkle
02 = Snow White	20 = Amber
03 = Cameo Ivory	21 = White Pearl
04 = Sunny Yellow	22 = Clear Frost
05 = Orange Poppy	23 = Berry Red
06 = Canyon Coral	24 = Ivy Green
07 = Cocoa Brown	
08 = Kelly Green	
09 = Emerald Green	
10 = Denim Blue	
11 = Blue Diamond	
12 = Royal Blue	
13 = Slate Blue	
14 = Amethyst	
15 = Ruby Red	
16 = Rose Quartz	
17 = Magenta Royal	
18 = Charcoal Black	

Other Supplies:

- Black transfer paper — for transferring designs to glass surfaces

- Cardboard — for making leading blank

- Craft knife — for trimming leading

- Craft stick — for mixing paint colors

- Foam cup — for combining paint colors

- Glass cleaner — for cleaning surfaces before leading is applied

- Lined notebook paper — for making straight lines of leading

- Non-stick plastic — for creating your own leading blank

- Nutpick or ice pick — for making a hole in the bottle tip

- Paper towels — for drying glass and wiping bottle tips and fingers

- Pencil — for tracing patterns

- Plain paper — for creating patterns to fit your window

- Scissors — for trimming leading and cutting out traced patterns

- Sharpened canyon — for drawing borders and connecting sections

- Soft bristle paint brush — for creating effects with Crystal Clear and Clear Frost paints

- Toothpicks — for combing out bubbles in paint

- Tracing paper — for tracing patterns and motifs from book

- White posterboard — for protecting work area

- Yardstick or ruler — for measuring and marking

Items to Decorate:

The projects in this book begin with your windows, including windows in doors and sidelights. The same designs can often be adapted to glass or plastic panels, framed or unframed, which hang in front of windows.

The home accessory projects are done on items you may have around the house or which you can purchase inexpensively. Most are clear glass or clear textured glass. They include bottles, jars, plates, clocks, candleholders and more.

Surface Preparation:

- Protect work surface with several layers of paper towels.

- Thoroughly clean outside and inside of the glass surface with glass cleaner, or wash with mild soap and water. Let dry.

- Trace pattern from the book. If size needs adjusting, use a photocopier to enlarge or reduce pattern.

- Apply pattern to project. Tape pattern behind or under glass of flat surfaces. It is sometimes possible to tape the trimmed pattern to the inside or backside of a three dimensional transparent project, but it is usually more effective to transfer the pattern onto the surface with black transfer paper.

Application Techniques

The application techniques shown in this chapter offer a variety of ways to create glass stain designs. The three techniques used to create these designs are the Vertical Technique, the Modular Technique, and the Horizontal Technique. Keep in mind the instructions listed on the right, before beginning any project.

Patterns can be reduced or enlarged on a copy machine as needed to fit the size of your window. To enlarge a pattern dimension, add border(s) or make the border(s) wider. To reduce a pattern dimension, trim borders or make them smaller.

1 Choose a design and colors for your room.

2 Measure your window(s) or surface and alter design (if necessary) to fit.

3 Draw or choose a pattern to fit your window.

4 Practice applying the leading strips on the surface you will be using. Get the feel of applying the paints. CAUTION: Always keep in mind that you are working on glass. Do not use excessive pressure when applying or removing materials.

How to Use the Vertical Technique

The Vertical Technique is used to create stain glass designs directly on windows and other vertical surfaces. For vertical application, allow two ounces of paint per square foot. (Coverage varies, depending on how thickly the paint is applied.)

Making Leading Strips

Leading strips must be prepared and dried before applying them to a vertical window. Leading cannot be squeezed directly onto a vertical surface. Here is how to make leading strips for application to a vertical surface.

1 Measure and add together the lengths of all the lines in the pattern. Multiply the total by the number of times the pattern will be repeated on your window(s).

2 Slip a piece of lined notebook paper under a leading blank (or place a piece of lined notebook paper on a piece of cardboard and cover with non-clinging plastic, such as a drycleaning bag). Make as many boards as you need for the project.

3 Remove simulated leading top and seal, then replace the top. Remove the small cap from the simulated leading bottle. Using a nutpick or ice pick, make a hole in the tip. Be certain the hole is large enough; small holes will not allow the leading to flow freely. Replace the cap. Hold the bottle upside down and tap firmly on a hard surface to force the leading into the tip. Remove small cap.

4 Hold the inverted bottle like a broom handle. Do not rest your elbow on your work surface—it will inhibit your movement. Squeeze lines of leading (⅛" to ³⁄₁₆" in diameter) on the leading blank or prepared board, following the notebook paper lines as guides. Let leading cure at least 72 hours until the strips peel up cleanly.

Making a Fine Line Tip

1 Make a hole in the tip according to label directions. Squeeze gently to dispense. Cut a 3½" strip of ¾" -wide cellophane tape. Place the left edge of the tape along the center of the tip. Press tape to spout as you rotate the bottle, securing the first turn of the tape and making a leak-proof seal. See Fig. 1.

2 Turn the bottle to form a cone with the tape. Press the tape firmly to the tip to prevent puckering. Continue turning the bottle, adhering the tape to previous layers. See Fig. 2.

3 The tape will reverse directions when the Fine Line Tip is formed. Continue to turn the bottle, allowing the tape to wind down. Press any extra tape over the side of the cap for easy removal later. To make a thicker line of leading, snip cone ⅛". See Fig. 3.

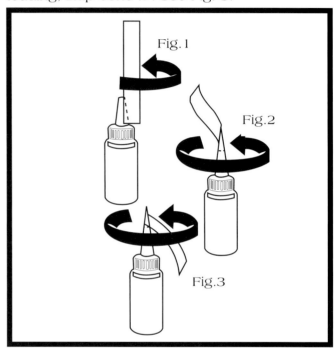

Fig. 1

Fig.2

Fig.3

Using Leading Strips to Outline the Design

TIPS:

• Trim blotches or irregularities from strips with small scissors before applying them.

• Do not pull or stretch the strips as you apply them. Do not handle the strips more than is necessary.

• Piece strips, if needed, by placing them end to end.

• Trim intersected lines neatly with a craft knife. Do not overlap the strips.

• Touch up gaps when you are finished by squeezing a small amount of simulated leading in gaps.

1 Thoroughly clean the inside and outside of the glass surface with glass cleaner or mild soap and water. Remove excess paint and/or glazing compound from the glass surface. Mask off window sill(s) and edges of window(s) that touch the glass. Place newspaper on the floor under window(s).

2 Tape your pattern on the outside of your window so you can see it from the inside. If you cannot access the outside of the window, transfer the pattern to the glass, using black transfer paper. You will also want to use black transfer paper if you are creating a mirror image design from a half-pattern.

3 Pull up the cured leading strips, working one strip at a time. Press leading strips to the window, following pattern lines. Continue until all pattern lines are covered with leading strips.

Painting the Design
TIPS:
• Do not shake the paint before applying—it will become too thin for vertical application.

• Use the tip to spread paint if it begins to run.

• Apply all paint directly from the bottle, except Clear Frost. Clear Frost is applied with a brush.

• Use less paint as you get to the bottom of a section; otherwise the paint may slide or droop.

• Immediately wash spilled paint off clothing, using soap and water. Do not allow it to dry.

• Immediately wipe spilled paint off window sill, sash, or frame with a damp rag. If paint dries on woodwork, spotting may result.

1 Begin in top left corner and run a thin line of paint across the top of the section, wiggling the tip back and forth as you move to the right. Repeat, moving side to side and downward, filling in one section at a time. Be certain to cover the corners and paint to the edge of the leading to seal the leading strips to the window and avoid light holes. Always complete an entire section before beginning another section or taking a break.

2 Immediately comb the wet paint with a toothpick, working back and forth to create smooth, even color and to pop the bubbles. For best results, comb all colored paints.

Painting Tips & Techniques

TIPS:

- All glass art paints have a milky appearance in the bottle and immediately after applying, but will become clear as they dry.

- Remove paint clogs by using a paper towel to push tip to one side and lift it out. Use nutpick or long pin to pull dried paint from inside. Replace tip and continue painting.

- Eliminate light holes in the corners of painted sections by dabbing some simulated leading over the hole. Simulated leading will be less noticeable than patching the gap with paint.

- Change a color before the paint dries, using a cotton swab to remove the unwanted color. Repaint.

- Intensify or darken a color by applying another layer of paint after the first layer dries.

- Lighten a paint color by mixing paint color with Crystal Clear.

- Create a translucent, not transparent look, by painting your design with Snow White, Canyon Coral, Cameo Ivory, or Rose Quartz. Although all glass art paints have a milky appearance in the bottle and until they are thoroughly dry, these four colors have a translucent appearance when dry.

Thinning Paint:

Use another bottle of paint and let the first one sit overnight if paint becomes too thin during application, or place it in the refrigerator for a short time. Do not allow to freeze.

Eliminating Holes:

Eliminate light holes in corners of painted sections by dabbing simulated leading over the hole. This method is less noticeable than recoating the section with paint.

Removing Design:

Use a craft knife to pry up the border. Start in one corner to remove an entire design from a project. Working toward the opposite corner, slowly peel the entire project from the glass. Most projects will peel off in one large piece.

Reducing Bubbles:

Peel out the bubble section and reapply paint. Comb with a toothpick while wet to minimize small bubbles and pop large ones.

Changing a Color:

Remove the dry paint to change the color of a section or fix a damaged area, using a single edge razor blade or craft knife to score the paint along the leading. Peel paint from surface with fingers. Clean the section, then reapply color.

Darkening a Color:

Apply more than one coat to intensify a color. Let each coat dry before applying the next to intensify a color.

Lightening a Color:

Mix paint with Crystal Clear paint to lighten a color. Pour the two colors of paint into a foam cup and mix with a craft stick, then pour the mixed color back into one of the bottles for application. Mixed paint should be allowed to sit overnight to "thicken up" again before applying.

Creating Even Colors:

Thoroughly comb the paint immediately after applying to smooth out bumps and distribute color evenly.

Creating Textures & Blends

Glass art paint creates a realistic look because of its thick consistency. All hand-rolled glass has texture, and glass art paint allows you to choose bumpy or smooth effects. Sponges, artist paint brushes, and small stencil brushes produce very different textured patterns. Following are some examples:

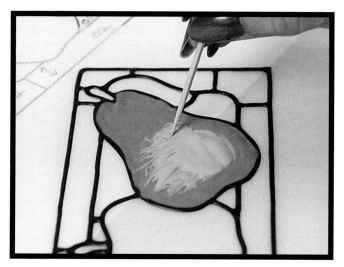

Shading:

Put two colors next to each other in the same section. Comb with a toothpick to blend the two together where they meet. This is perfect for flower petals, leaves, and fruits.

Cathedral Texture:

Begin at the top left of a section and run thin lines of paint from left to right, working top to bottom until the section is painted for the look of clear cathedral glass. This creates a uniformly bumpy texture which distorts images, but allows maximum light to pass through the glass.

Feathery Frost:

Apply Crystal Clear paint with a soft bristle brush, using a light touch to create the feathery look of frost on a winter's day. Pour some paint into a shallow cup and dip the tips of the bristles into the paint. Beginning at the top of a section, make a comma stroke to the right, then one to the left. Continue in rows until the section is painted, applying the paint onto the edges of the leading to secure the design to the surface. This is an economical way to cover a large area.

Opalescent:

Create an opalescent look with translucent colors, such as Snow White marbleized with one or more colors. Place drops of one color in an area, then fill in with Snow White translucent color. Use the bottle tip or a toothpick to swirl the two colors. Do not comb or over-mix. Pop only larger bubbles.

13

Smooth Frost:

Dab Clear Frost paint on the surface with a soft bristle brush, covering the section with a thin coat for a smooth, frosted look. Brush the paint up onto the leading to seal it in place. The frosted look will appear as the paint dries.

Finishing the Design

Curing and Cleaning:

- Glass art projects usually dry in eight hours and cure in three to seven days. Protect projects from moisture while curing. Drying times vary due to humidity, temperature, and thickness of paint.

- Once glass art paint cures, it will withstand cold temperatures unless moisture condenses on the window and freezes. If freeze damage occurs, the area can be repaired. Use a craft knife to score the paint in the damaged section, lift, remove, and repaint.

- Let your project cure at least one week before cleaning. To clean, spray a light mist of water on a soft cloth.

Wipe the surface gently with the cloth to remove dust. Do not use an excessive amount of water, solvent-based cleaners, or abrasive cleaning products. All will harm your design.

Removing Glass Art Designs:

Cut the paint layer with a craft knife where it meets the leaded lines to remove a section of a glass art design. Lift. To remove a whole window, cut the paint where it meets the frame of the window sash and peel off the entire design.

Other Items to Decorate:

- Mirrors mounted in small bathrooms or on chests of drawers

- Decorative round glassware, such as canisters, votives, and plates

- Cabinet doors, hutch doors, and folding screens

- Window toppers on window walls, such as 12"-wide border across the expanse of the windows, leaving the bottom area plain if you want to maintain a view

How to Use the Modular Technique

The Modular Technique is an alternate way to create designs on vertical surfaces. The design motifs are leaded, painted, and cured on a plastic surface; then peeled up, and adhered to the window. Then the background is painted, using the Vertical Technique. With the Modular Technique, you can create an intricate pattern in less time because much of the work is done horizontally.

Using Leading Blanks

1 Plan design by first cutting apart pattern pieces. Tape pieces on window as desired.

Use black transfer paper to roughly trace the outline of each pattern piece. These will be your guide to later place painted pieces. Use a sharpened crayon to draw borders, branches or connecting lines between sections. Remove pattern pieces.

2 Prepare leading blank by placing the smooth side up. Place pattern pieces under leading blank as close together as possible, but not overlapping.

14

Applying Simulated Leading to Design Motifs

1 Remove the cap from the simulated leading bottle. Using a nutpick or ice pick, make a hole in the tip. Be certain the hole is large enough; small holes will not allow the leading to flow freely. Replace the cap. Hold the bottle upside down and tap firmly on a hard surface to force the leading into the tip. Remove cap.

2 See "How to Use the Vertical Technique" on pages 9-14. Do not rest your elbow on your work surface—it will inhibit your movement. Squeeze lines of leading (⅛" to ³⁄₁₆" in diameter) on the leading blank or prepared board, following the leading lines of the design motif. When you get near the end of your pattern line, stop squeezing and lower the bottle tip to the plastic surface. (This way you will not have blobs of leading when you stop and start.) Let leading dry 24 hours before painting.

Correcting Leading Mistakes

Correct leading mistakes on leading blank material by letting leading dry, pulling up any unwanted leading and snipping off or trimming with small scissors. Place the leading back on the leading blank. Press firmly in place.

Correct leading mistakes on plastic-covered cardboard by removing unwanted leading mistakes inside the design motif with a cotton swab while the leading is still wet. You can trim mistakes outside the design motif with scissors after the cured, completed motif is pulled up.

Using Leading Strips for Connecting the Design

1 Measure and add together the lengths of the remaining leading lines (ones that are not part of design motifs).

2 See "Making Leading Strips" on page 9. Make enough leading lines to complete your window. Let cure at least 72 hours.

Painting the Design

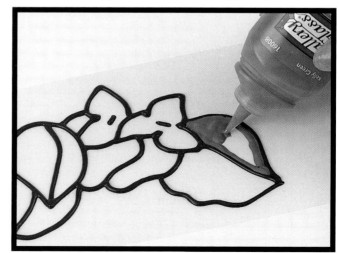

1 Hold the bottle upside down and squeeze the color around the edges of the design motif. Fill in the center of the design motif with paint. Apply paint liberally, at about the same depth as the leading. Be certain the paint fills the corners of the design. If the paint is too thin, the cured design motif could tear when you pull it off the plastic.

2 Immediately comb the wet paint with a toothpick, working back and forth to create smooth, even color and to pop the bubbles. Be certain to make the final combing in the direction you want the texture to be.

3 Remove bubbles by tapping underneath the painted area with the bowl of a teaspoon or the end of a pencil. You will have to tap more firmly if you use the plastic-covered cardboard than if you use a leading blank sheet. NEVER use the tapping technique on glass; the glass could shatter.

4 Let the design motifs cure for 24 to 48 hours on a dry, flat surface with good air circulation. (The top of the refrigerator is a good place.) Drying time varies, depending on the thickness of the paint and the humidity. The paint will be transparent when dry.

Completing the Design on the Window

Wait for a dry day to complete your glass art project. Rainy days and high humidity can cause problems. Even if your windows are dry to the touch, having too much moisture in the air can keep the paint from drying indefinitely, because moisture will get trapped under the paint.

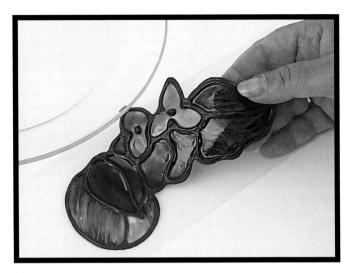

1 Gently peel the design motifs off the leading blank sheet or the plastic-covered cardboard.

2 Position the design motifs on the window, using your pattern as a guide for placement. Place larger elements, such as flowers, first; place smaller elements, such as leaves and stems, next. Be careful not to stretch the design motifs or get the backs of them dirty or dusty. Excessive handling can keep the motifs from adhering properly. Continue until all design motifs are in position.

3 Add the cured, straight leading strips to connect the design motifs to one another and to connect the motifs with the edges of the window. The leading curves easily, not requiring the connecting lines to be straight.

4 Touch up any gaps in the leading by squeezing small amounts of simulated leading in the gaps. Let dry.

5 Paint the background areas of the design. See "Painting the Design" on page 11. Most often, the background is filled in with Crystal Clear. Be certain the paint covers the edges of the leading to completely seal the surface.

If the window you would like to decorate is not suitable for the Vertical Technique because of moisture or temperature problems, you can create a glass art design to hang in front of the window or to mount onto a window.

Hanging Plastic Panels

Paint a panel on plastic and then hang in front of the window. Paint cannot be removed from plastic surfaces when dry. Plastic panels can be purchased at home improvement centers or hardware stores and cut to size. The panel should be smaller than the glass area of the window to allow circulation behind the panel. Unlike glass, they can be drilled and hung without a frame. To hang, drill holes in the panel before painting. After paint is dry, suspend the panel from the window frame, using cup hooks and thin chain, monofilament line, or ribbon.

Mounting Plastic

Mount a plastic panel into a window sill by using glazing points to hold in place in front of the glass. Allow some extra space for air circulation to prevent moisture behind panels. For a more realistic look, cover the edge of the panel with simulated leading after hanging.

Using Glass Panels

Paint your designs on glass, then frame them. The framed designs can be hung in front of your windows.

Using the Horizontal Technique

1 Choose a design and alter the pattern, if necessary, to fit your panel.

2 Gather supplies. (For Horizontal Technique, allow at least 2 oz. of paint per square foot of panel.)

3 Cover your work surface. Place the pattern under the panel.

4 Squeeze simulated leading directly onto the panel over the pattern lines. (It is not necessary to make separate leading strips—just squeeze the simulated leading in place.) Let dry 24 hours.

5 Apply paint to one section of the design at a time. See "Painting the Design" on page 11.

6 Immediately comb the wet paint with a toothpick, working back and forth to create smooth, even color and to pop the bubbles. Bubbles are more prevalent with horizontal application; combing in several directions can help control them. Be certain to make the final combing in the direction you want the texture to be. On plastic panels or plastic-covered cardboard, you can also remove bubbles by tapping underneath the section with the bowl of a teaspoon. NEVER use the tapping technique on glass; the glass could shatter.

Small Glass Art Projects

Using the Vertical Technique, leading lines are made separately and allowed to dry. The precured strips are pressed onto the glass project. The item is then painted in an upright position.

Leading the Design Using the Vertical Technique

1 Use a piece of lined notebook paper for a pattern. Place a leading blank over the paper. You will be able to see and follow the lines of the notebook paper as you lead. Estimate the number of feet of leading you will need by measuring the leading lines on your pattern. Hold the inverted bottle like a broom handle. As leading begins to flow, touch the leading (not the bottle tip) where you want the line to begin. Raise the tip slightly above the surface and move along the pattern lines. The cord of leading will drape down onto the pattern line. To stop, lower tip to surface. Lead across the notebook paper lines. Make enough lines to complete your project. Let leading dry at least 72 hours, longer if humidity is high, or until leading lines will peel up cleanly.

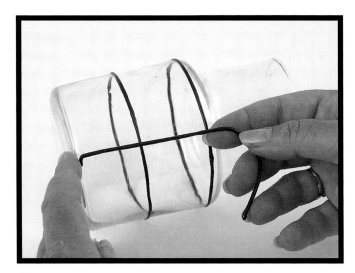

2 Trim any blotches or irregularities from leading strips before applying them to project. Peel up the cured leading strips and press them onto the clean glass, covering the pattern lines. Do not stretch strips as you apply them, or handle them any more than necessary. If a pattern line is longer than your strip, strips can be pieced together by placing them end to end. Trim intersecting lines with a craft knife so that they meet cleanly. Do not overlap leading strips. Touch up gaps, if needed, by squeezing in small amounts of leading.

Painting the Design Using the Vertical Technique

1 Apply glass art paint from the bottle onto upright item, one section at a time. Hold bottle tip against the glass and squeeze gently. Start in the top left corner of the section. Run a thin line of paint across the section onto glass. Be certain to cover the corners. Move the bottle back and forth, working downward in horizontal rows. If the paint begins to run, you are applying too much. Use the bottle tip to spread it thinner. Use less paint toward the bottom of the section because the paint above it may slide downward slightly.

2 Use a toothpick or nutpick to comb the paint to minimize bubbles, to evenly distribute color, and to give a grain or a directional texture to the design. Hold the toothpick perpendicular to the glass. Starting at the top of the section, streak the tip back and forth all the way to the bottom. Comb similar sections in the same direction. Do not comb Crystal Clear sections. Leave these bumpy or otherwise textured.

3 Remove large bubbles by popping with a toothpick or using the bottle tip for suction. Ignore small bubbles. They will add to the realistic look.

4 Let project dry. Glass art projects usually dry in eight hours and cure in three to seven days. Protect your project from moisture while it is curing.

5 Let project cure at least one week before cleaning. To clean, spray a light mist of water on a soft cloth. Wipe the surface gently with the cloth to remove dust. Do not use an excessive amount of water, solvent-based cleaners, or abrasive cleaning products. All will harm your design. Never submerge the project or put it in the dishwasher.

Using the Modular Technique, the designs are leaded and painted on a leading blank. After drying, it is peeled up and placed onto the object being decorated. It is self-adhering. If desired, a clear or colored painted background can be added by the Vertical or Horizontal Techniques.

Leading the Design Using the Modular Technique

1 Position patterns by placing them under a leading blank or place them on a piece of cardboard and cover with non-clinging plastic.

2 Squeeze leading out along pattern lines. On a separate leading blank, make some straight leading lines to act as connectors for designs, if needed. Let leading dry eight hours before painting the design.

Painting the Design Using the Modular Technique

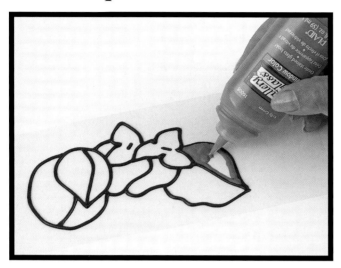

1 Flow paint from the bottle directly onto the leading blank within each section. Paint around the perimeter of the section first, then fill in the center of that section. Apply paint liberally—to about the same depth as the leading. If paint is too thin, the cured design may tear when being removed from the leading blank. Use a toothpick to evenly distribute the paint in the section.

2 Comb the paint to remove bubbles. Hold the leading blank firmly in your non-painting hand and tap directly under the combed section with a pencil or teaspoon. (If using plastic-covered cardboard, tap more firmly.)

3 Let project dry for 24 to 48 hours on a dry, flat surface with good air circulation, such as the top of the refrigerator. All cloudy areas must turn transparent before proceeding.

Adhere the Design & Finish Project

1 Peel up the modular designs and place them in the desired location on your glass item. Position larger elements first, then smaller ones. Be careful not to stretch the designs or soil the backs of them. Press them on from the center outward to minimize air bubbles. These designs will be self-adhering.

2 Use precured leading strips as needed to connect the modular elements of the design. See "How to Use the Vertical Technique" on page 9. Place these strips directly onto the glass item. Separate the background into segments as needed with precured leading strips. Touch up any gaps in the leading with simulated leading and let spots dry thoroughly before applying paint to the background.

3 If background painting is desired, such as a clear background or a color, see "Painting Tips & Techniques" on page 12. Apply background paint over the perimeter leading around modular design to completely seal the surface. Adding a background finishes off the entire design, see "Making Window Scenes" on page 70.

Total Window Designs

A stained glass window is a spectacular decorator touch. Designs created with glass art paint have the same enchantment of authentic stained glass art at a fraction of the cost, time, and effort. Whether regular windows, door windows, sidelights, or other windowed areas, these designs can make them special.

Using Patterns

For some patterns in this book, one-fourth or one-half of the design is printed. The diagram on the right shows how to complete the design, using a one-fourth pattern.

To create a mirror image, create a pattern on tracing paper to fit half the window. Hold the pattern up to the window and trace the design on the back of the tracing paper. When you transfer the pattern to the window, use black transfer paper and transfer half the pattern at a time.

TIPS:

• Control the humidity as much as possible in your home after your painted windows have dried. High humidity and rainy days can make glass paints look cloudy (especially the Crystal Clear paint). Once the humidity drops, the cloudiness will go away. Air circulation and warmer air are conducive to clearer windows. Open bathroom doors after showers, use central heat and air rather than space heat, and do not open your windows in humid weather. You can also use a hair dryer to clear a window—set the dryer on its lowest setting and, holding it 6-10" from the surface, move the air across the window until it clears.

• Wait for a dry day to create a project. Rainy days and high humidity can cause problems. Even if your windows are dry to the touch, having too much moisture in the air can keep the paint from drying indefinitely, because moisture will get trapped under the paint.

¼ of Pattern

Victorian Sunflower

The Victorian Sunflower design is great above shutters or under mini-blinds. Leaves can be used in all corners or only in the lower corners.

GATHER THESE SUPPLIES

2 oz. Glass Paint:
03 = Cameo Ivory
07 = Cocoa Brown
08 = Kelly Green
13 = Slate Blue
20 = Amber
22 = Clear Frost
24 = Ivy Green

INSTRUCTIONS

Prepare:
1. See "Surface Preparation" on page 8. Prepare glass surface.

2. See "Patterns" on page 7. Prepare pattern.

Apply:
3. See "How to Use the Vertical Technique" on pages 9-14. Apply simulated leading to create leading strips. Apply leading strips to window, following pattern. Paint surface with glass paint, using the Vertical Technique.

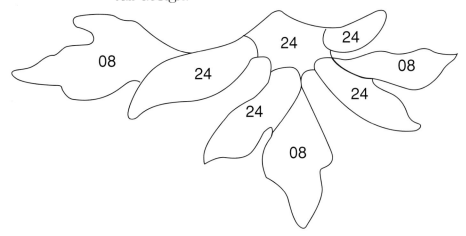

Enlarge 175%   Use mirror image and inverted pattern for full design.

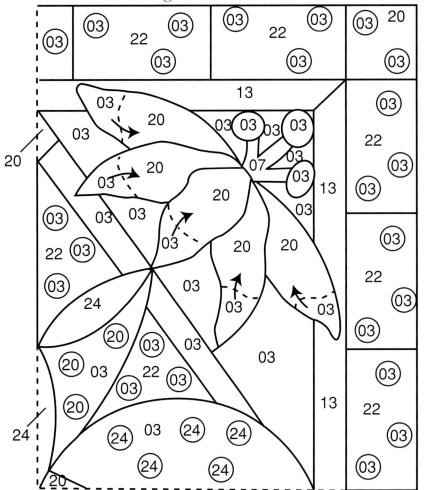

Enlarge 175%   Substitute for flower in panel. Use mirror image and inverted pattern for full design.

Lattice Gazebo

Pictured on pages 24-25.

The latticework borders at the top and bottom of each sash enhance the gazebo feeling of this octagonal breakfast room. The center areas can be left unpainted to expose an attractive view.

GATHER THESE SUPPLIES

2 oz. Glass Paint:
01 = Crystal Clear (8 oz.)
02 = Snow White
03 = Cameo Ivory

INSTRUCTIONS

Prepare:
1. See "Surface Preparation" on page 8. Prepare glass surface.

2. See "Patterns" on page 7. Prepare pattern.

Apply:
3. See "How to Use the Vertical Technique" on pages 9-14. Apply simulated leading to create leading strips. Apply leading strips to window, following pattern. Paint surface with glass paint, using the Vertical Technique.

Enlarge 210%   Repeat as needed to make top and bottom borders.

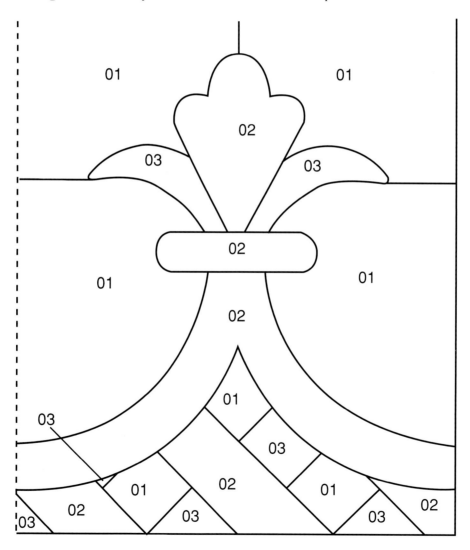

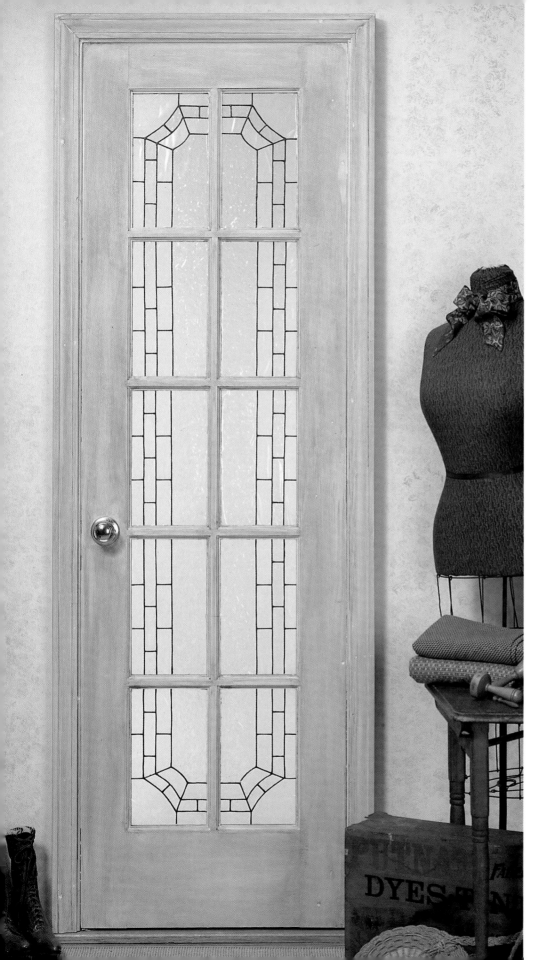

Classic French Door

The corners of this design can be adapted to fit almost any size pane. Remaining outer panes should be filled in with straight border sections. If your door has three or more panes in each row, fill the center ones with Crystal Clear glass art paint.

GATHER THESE SUPPLIES

2 oz. Glass Paint:
01 = Crystal Clear (8 oz.)
22 = Clear Frost

INSTRUCTIONS

Prepare:
1. See "Surface Preparation" on page 8. Prepare glass surface.

2. See "Patterns" on page 7. Prepare pattern.

Apply:
3. See "How to Use the Vertical Technique" on pages 9-14. Apply simulated leading to create leading strips. Apply leading strips to window, following pattern. Paint surface with glass paint, using the Vertical Technique.

Enlarge 150%   Repeat straight border on inside, top, and
bottom outer panes.

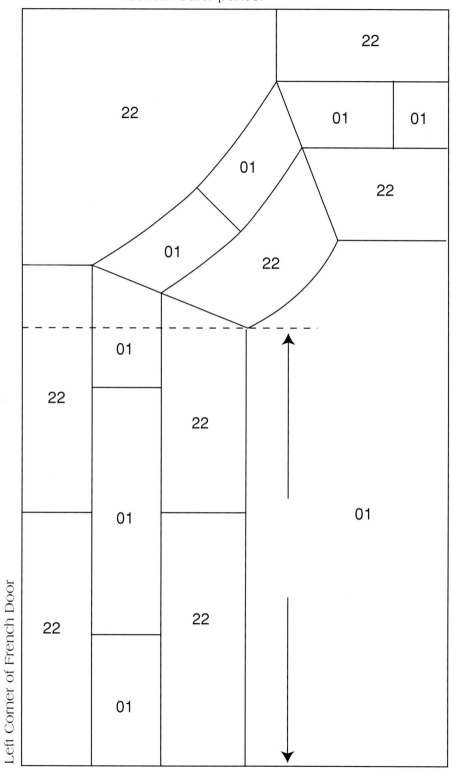

Victorian Bouquet

Pictured on page 29.

This design can be repeated to make a border on any size window or patio door. In this case, the design was repeated twice across the top and bottom and used once on each side. The center motifs are adapted from the border design.

GATHER THESE SUPPLIES

2 oz. Glass Paint:
01 = Crystal Clear (8 oz.)
02 = Snow White
08 = Kelly Green
11 = Blue Diamond
14 = Amethyst
16 = Rose Quartz
18 = Charcoal Black
22 = Clear Frost
23 = Berry Red
24 = Ivy Green

INSTRUCTIONS

Prepare:
1. See "Surface Preparation" on page 8. Prepare glass surface.

2. See "Patterns" on page 7. Prepare pattern.

Apply:
3. See "How to Use the Vertical Technique" on pages 9-14. Apply simulated leading to create leading strips. Apply leading strips to window, following pattern. Paint surface with glass paint, using the Vertical Technique.

Enlarge 230%

Fleur di Lis Window & Palladian Arch

Pictured on page 31.

This combination shows the versatility of glass art designs. The Palladian Arch was used above the Fleur di Lis Window. For the window, the border design was repeated several times at the window top and bottom. To create the diamonds, draw crossed diagonal lines to fill the remaining space on your windows.

Palladian windows vary in size. The pattern and its mirror image can be used across the top of any large window, patio door, or window wall; or it can be enlarged to fit a half-circle window like this one.

GATHER THESE SUPPLIES

2 oz. Glass Paint for Fleur di Lis Window:
03 = Cameo Ivory
19 = Gold Sparkle
22 = Clear Frost

2 oz. Glass Paint for Palladian Arch:
01 = Crystal Clear (8 oz.)
05 = Orange Poppy
19 = Gold sparkle

22 = Clear Frost
24 = Ivy Green

INSTRUCTIONS

Prepare:
1. See "Surface Preparation" on page 8. Prepare glass surface.

2. See "Patterns" on page 7. Prepare pattern.

Apply:
3. See "How to Use the Vertical Technique" on pages 9-14. Apply simulated leading to create leading strips. Apply leading strips to window, following pattern. Paint surface with glass paint, using the Vertical Technique.

Enlarge 235%   Repeat to fit width of window. Invert for top border.

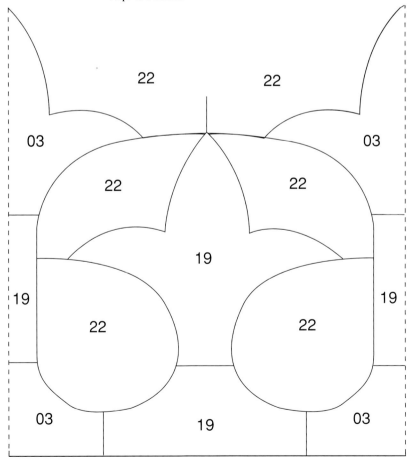

Enlarge 195%

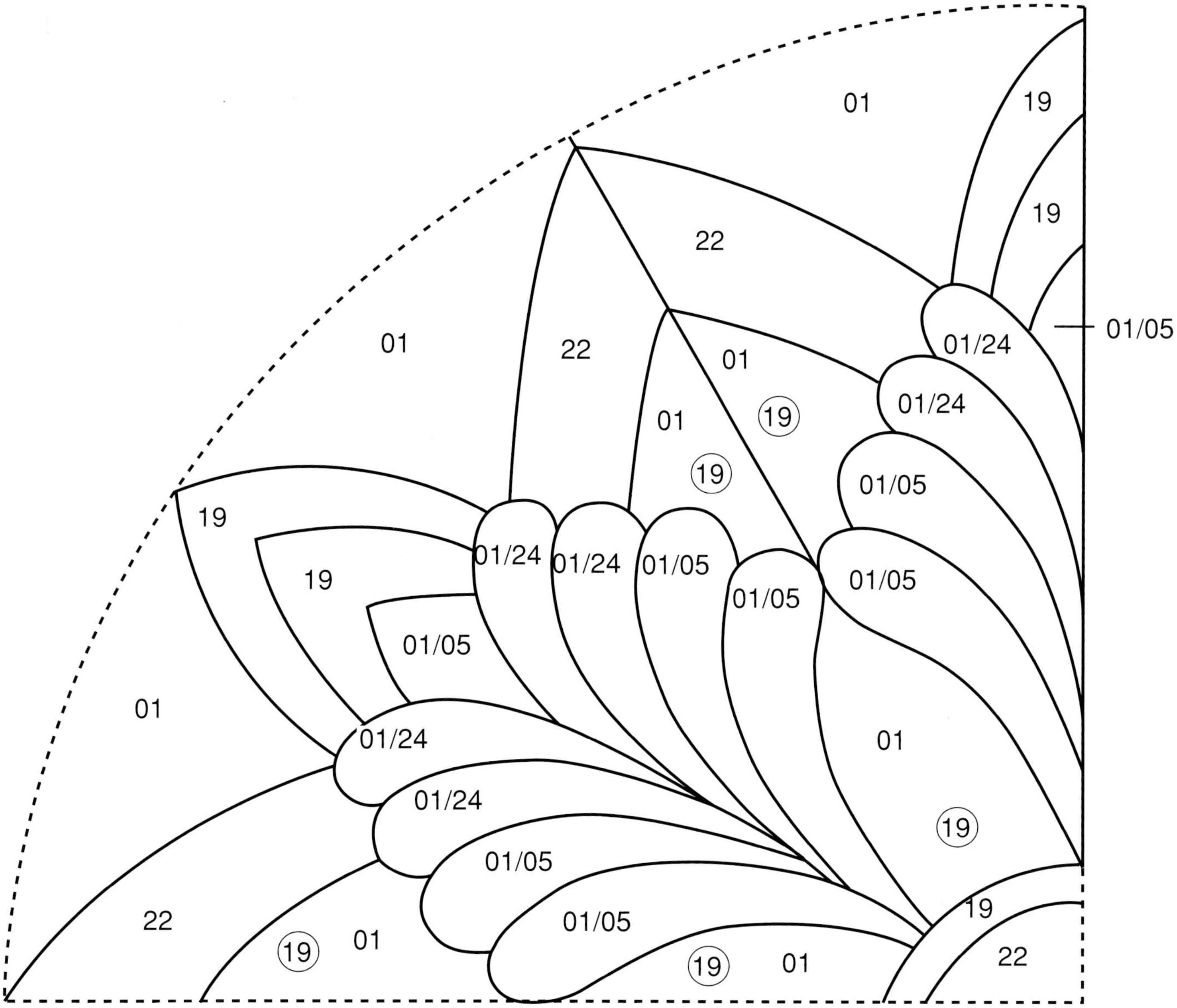

01 19 19

01 22 01/05

01 22 01 01/24

01 01 (19) 01/24

01/05

19 (19) 01/24 01/24 01/05 01/05

19 01/24 01/05 01/05

01/05 01/05

01 01/24

01/24 01

01/05 (19)

01/05 19

22 (19) 01 (19) 01 22

33

Country Tulips

Cheerful yellow tulips accented with blue are a sunny accent. Use the complete tulip design on the top half of the window. Invert the design and use the mirror image for the bottom half.

GATHER THESE SUPPLIES

2 oz. Glass Paint:
01 = Crystal Clear (8 oz.)
02 = Snow White
04 = Sunny Yellow
10 = Denim Blue
13 = Slate Blue
22 = Clear Frost

INSTRUCTIONS

Prepare:
1. See "Surface Preparation" on page 8. Prepare glass surface.

2. See "Patterns" on page 7. Prepare pattern.

Apply:
3. See "How to Use the Vertical Technique" on pages 9-14. Apply simulated leading to create leading strips. Apply leading strips to window, following pattern. Paint surface with glass paint, using the Vertical Technique.

Enlarge 175%   Use mirror image for right side.

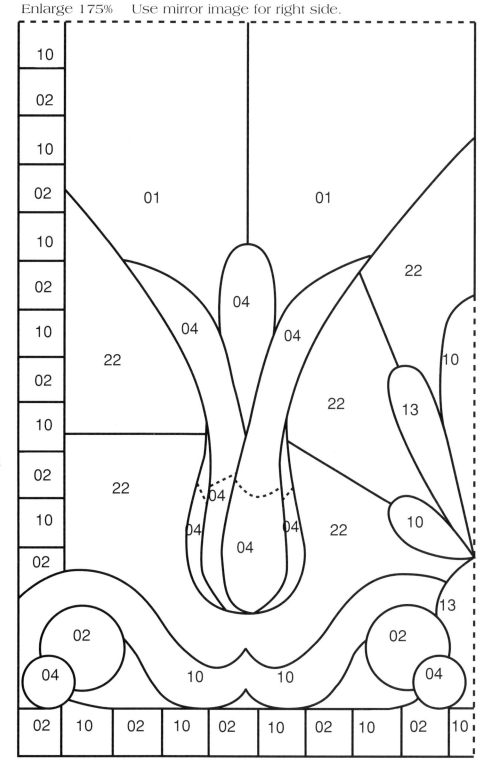

Water Lilies

The Water Lilies design elements can be repeated or overlapped. A simple border finishes the window.

GATHER THESE SUPPLIES

2 oz. Glass Paint:
01 = Crystal Clear (8 oz.)
08 = Kelly Green
16 = Rose Quartz
23 = Berry Red
24 = Ivy Green

INSTRUCTIONS

Prepare:
1. See "Surface Preparation" on page 8. Prepare glass surface.

2. See "Patterns" on page 7. Prepare patterns.

Apply:
3. See "How to Use the Modular Technique" on pages 14-16. Apply simulated leading to leading blank. Paint leading blank with glass paint, using the Modular Technique. Apply design to glass surface.

Enlarge 140%

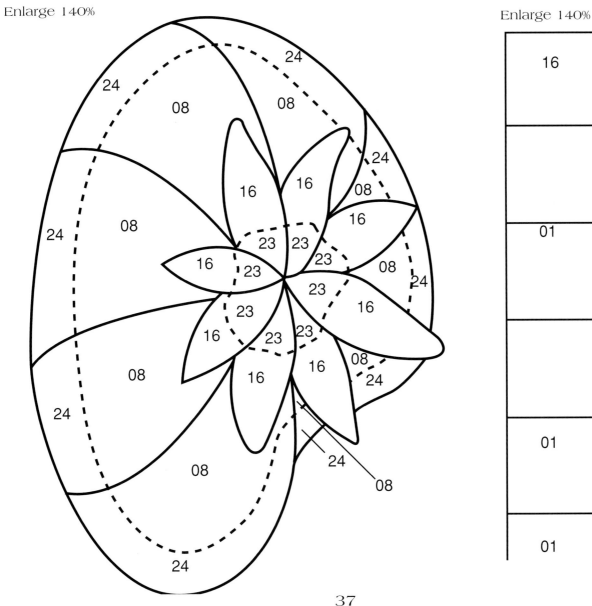

Enlarge 140%

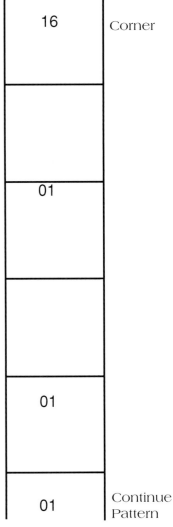

Pattern Actual Size

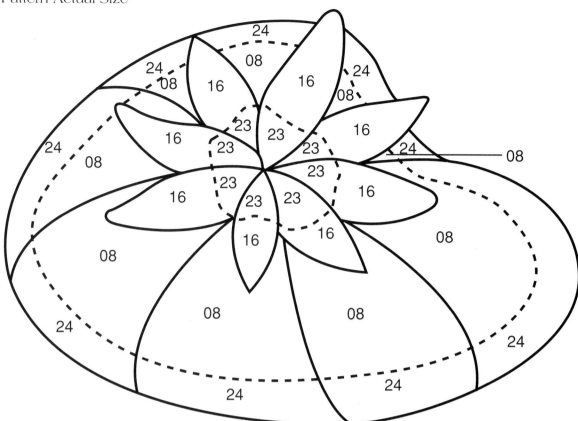

Pattern Actual Size

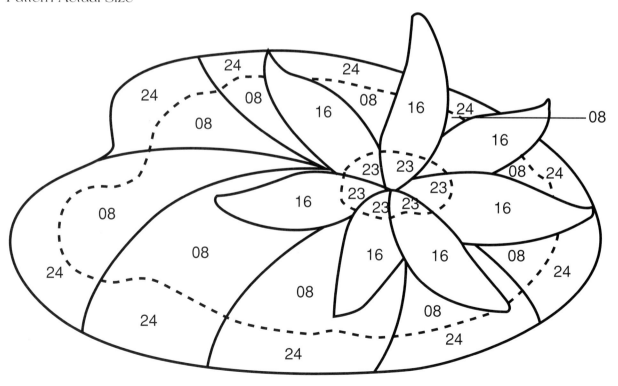

38

Victorian Swirl

Pictured on page 39.

The Victorian Swirl pattern was enlarged so the width fits the dimensions of these bedroom windows. An extra white border was added at top and bottom to fill the remaining space.

GATHER THESE SUPPLIES

2 oz. Glass Paint:

01 = Crystal Clear
02 = Snow White
10 = Denim Blue
19 = Gold Sparkle
22 = Clear Frost

INSTRUCTIONS

Prepare:

1. See "Surface Preparation" on page 8. Prepare glass surface.

2. See "Patterns" on page 7. Prepare pattern.

Apply:

3. See "How to Use the Vertical Technique" on pages 9-14. Apply simulated leading to create leading strips. Apply leading strips to window, following pattern. Paint surface with glass paint, using the Vertical Technique.

Enlarge 155%   Invert for upper sash.

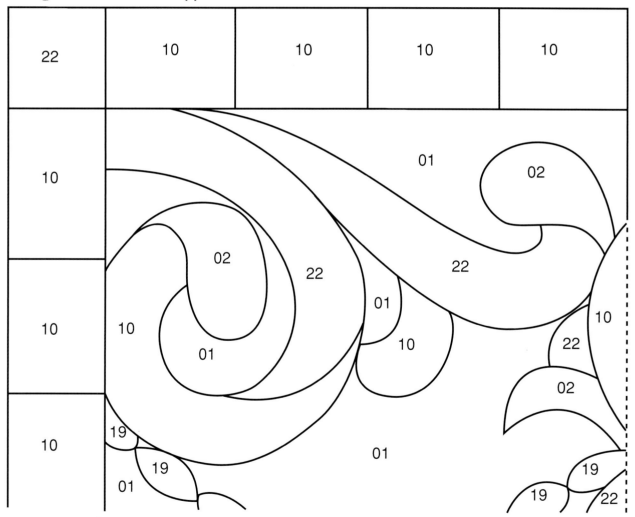

Enlarge 155%   Invert for upper sash.

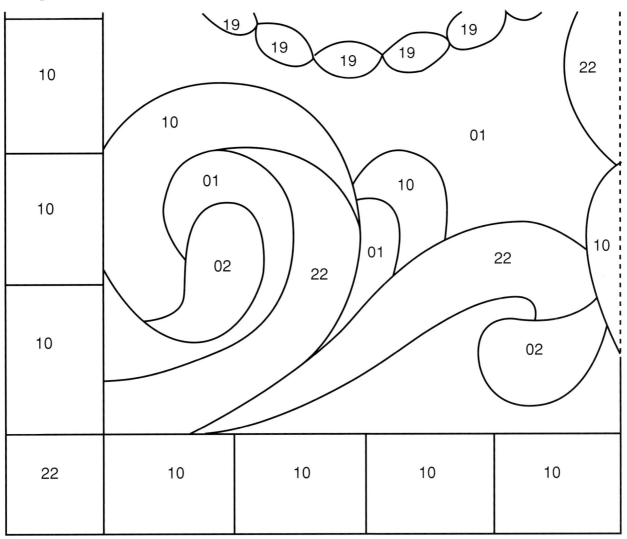

Country Victorian Window

This design uses a mirror image to fill the entire window. Make two sets and apply them to top and bottom of your window. The elements of the design will fit within any existing mullions, or you could create your own as we did. If your windows currently have four panes across (or the window is too large to divide it into only three panes), divide the center medallion in half so that it straddles the center mullion or lead line. Create extra simulated leading strips to connect all elements in the design, applying them in curved arcs as the pattern shows.

GATHER THESE SUPPLIES

2 oz. Glass Paint:
03 = Cameo Ivory
06 = Canyon Coral
16 = Rose Quartz

INSTRUCTIONS

Prepare:
1. See "Surface Preparation" on page 8. Prepare glass surface.

2. See "Patterns" on page 7. Prepare pattern.

Apply:
3. See "How to Use the Modular Technique" on pages 14-16. Apply simulated leading to leading blank. Paint leading blank with glass paint, using the Modular Technique. Apply design to glass surface.

Enlarge 140%   Repeat pattern upside down for bottom of design. Reserve pattern for other side.

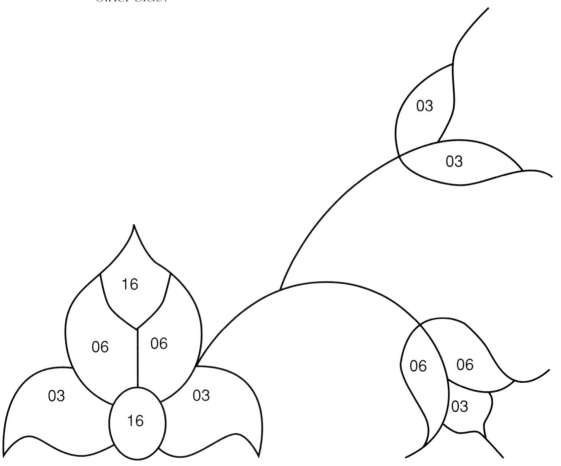

Floral Ovals

These ovals fit into any existing mullions. You can also create your own mullions, using simulated leading. If your mullions extend three across instead of four, choose just three of the floral designs. This design makes a nice top design for typical windows; keep the lower portion of the window clear or fill in with Crystal Clear glass paint for more privacy.

GATHER THESE SUPPLIES

2 oz. Glass Paint for Iris:
03 = Cameo Ivory
04 = Sunny Yellow
08 = Kelly Green
14 = Amethyst

2 oz. Glass Paint for Rose:
03 = Cameo Ivory
08 = Kelly Green
16 = Rose Quartz

2 oz. Glass Paint for Columbine:
03 = Cameo Ivory
04 = Sunny Yellow
08 = Kelly Green
12 = Royal Blue
21 = White Pearl

2 oz. Glass Paint for Tulips:
03 = Cameo Ivory
04 = Sunny Yellow
08 = Kelly Green
15 = Ruby Red

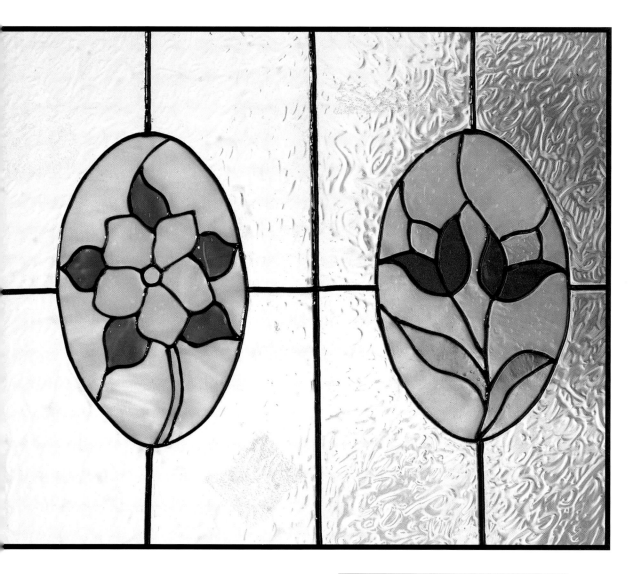

INSTRUCTIONS

Prepare:

1. See "Surface Preparation" on page 8. Prepare glass surface.

2. See "Patterns" on page 7. Prepare patterns.

Apply:

3. See "How to Use the Modular Technique" on pages 14-16. Apply simulated leading to leading blank. Paint leading blank with glass paint, using the Modular Technique. Apply design to glass surface.

Idea for Placement

45

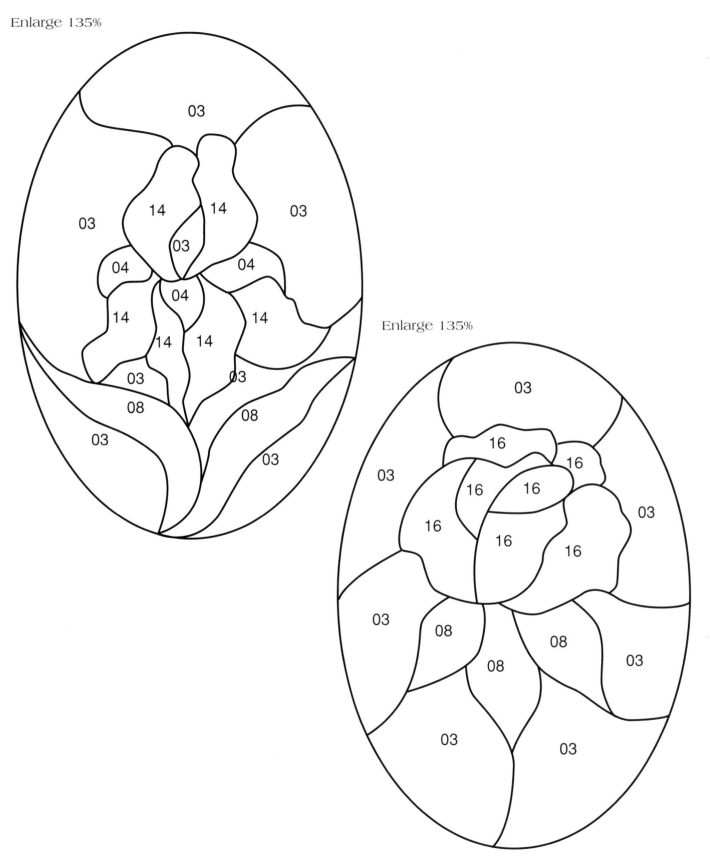

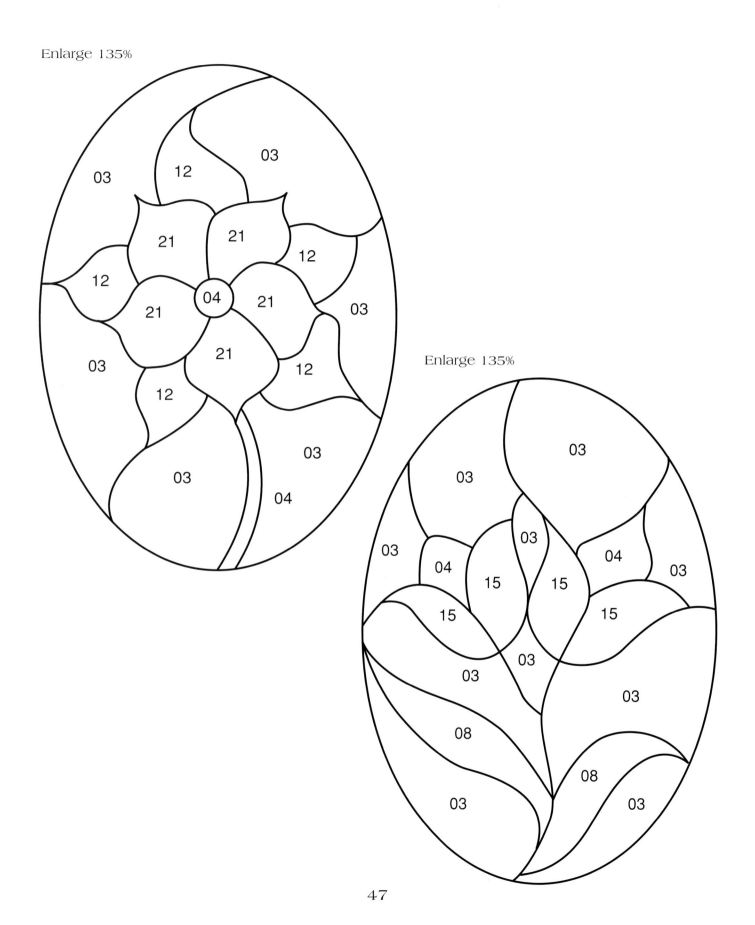

Enlarge 135%

03
12
03
21 21
12
12
21 04 21
03
21
03
12
12
03
03
04

Enlarge 135%

03
03
03
03
04
04
03
15 15
03
15
15
15
03
03
03
08
03
08
03
03

47

Geometric Bay Window

The areas using Clear Frost were applied with a brush for a relatively smooth texture. The areas of Crystal Clear were applied from the bottle for a cathedral texture.

GATHER THESE SUPPLIES

2 oz. Glass Paint:
01 = Crystal Clear
22 = Clear Frost

INSTRUCTIONS

Prepare:
1. See "Surface Preparation" on page 8. Prepare glass surface.

2. See "Patterns" on page 7. Prepare patterns.

Apply:
3. See "How to Use the Vertical Technique" on pages 9-14. Apply simulated leading to create leading strips. Apply leading strips to window, following pattern. Paint surface with glass paint, using the Vertical Technique.

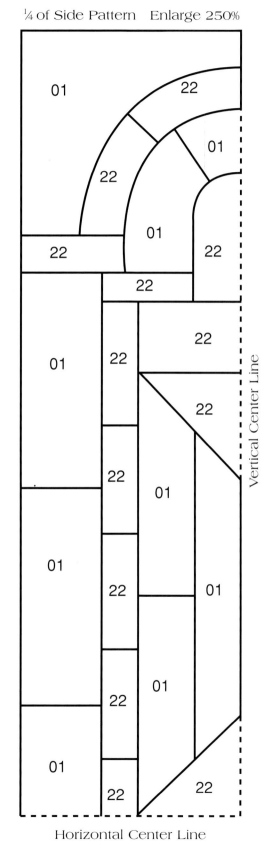

¼ of Side Pattern   Enlarge 250%

Vertical Center Line

Horizontal Center Line

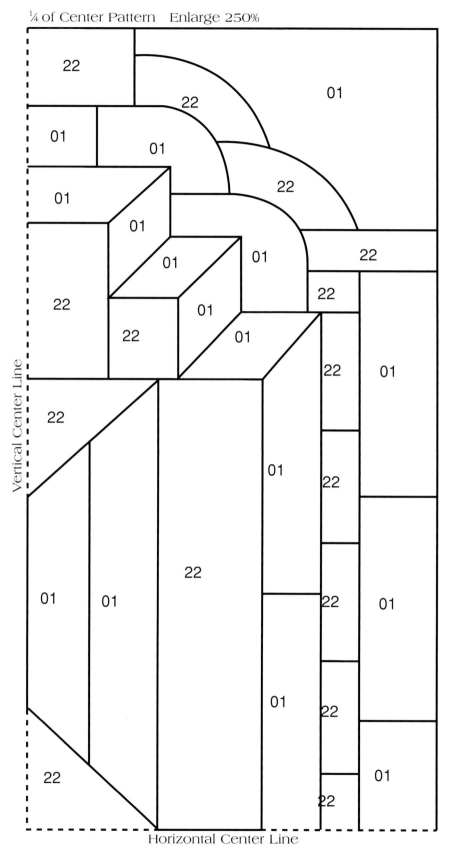

Ovals & Diamonds

Pictured on page 51.

You will love combining Clear Frost with the cathedral texture of Crystal Clear for a more elegant, upscale look. This master bedroom window has 12 panes, 7½" x 9" and a palladian of 4 panes, 9" x 11". The colorless, textured areas are contrasted with ovals of marbleized Emerald Green and Snow White.

GATHER THESE SUPPLIES

2 oz. Glass Paint:
01 = Crystal Clear
02 = Snow White
09 = Emerald Green
22 = Clear Frost

INSTRUCTIONS

Prepare:
1. See "Surface Preparation" on page 8. Prepare glass surface.

2. See "Patterns" on page 7. Prepare pattern.

Apply:
3. See "How to Use the Vertical Technique" on pages 9-14. Apply simulated leading to create leading strips. Apply leading strips to window, following pattern. Paint surface with glass paint, using the Vertical Technique.

Enlarge 160%

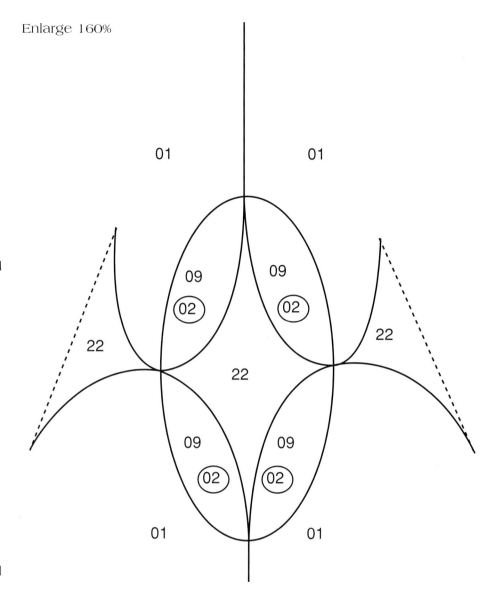

Enlarge 160%

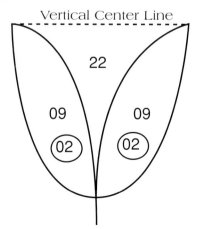

Beautiful Symmetry Sidelights

Pictured on page 53.

This design coordinates a glass entry door with sidelights. Clear Frost is applied with a brush and Crystal Clear is applied from the bottle for the cathedral texture. The colorless, textured areas are contrasted with smaller Emerald Green sections combed for texture.

GATHER THESE SUPPLIES

2 oz. Glass Paint:
01 = Crystal Clear
09 = Emerald Green
22 = Clear Frost

INSTRUCTIONS

Prepare:
1. See "Surface Preparation" on page 8. Prepare glass surface.

2. See "Patterns" on page 7. Prepare pattern.

Apply:
3. See "How to Use the Vertical Technique" on pages 9-14. Apply simulated leading to create leading strips. Apply leading strips to window, following pattern. Paint surface with glass paint, using the Vertical Technique.

½ of Sidelight Pattern   Enlarge 140%

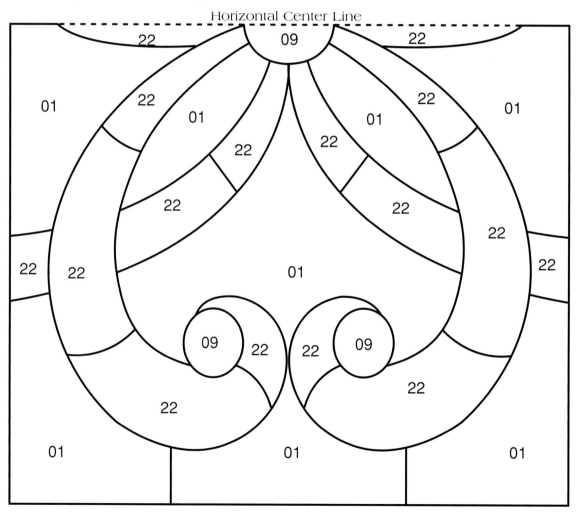

54

Beautiful Symmetry Entry

Pictured on page 53.

This entry door design coordinates with the sidelight design on page 54.

GATHER THESE SUPPLIES

2 oz. Glass Paint:
01 = Crystal Clear
09 = Emerald Green
22 = Clear Frost

INSTRUCTIONS

Prepare:

1. See "Surface Preparation" on page 8. Prepare glass surface.

2. See "Patterns" on page 7. Prepare pattern.

Apply:

3. See "How to Use the Vertical Technique" on pages 9-14. Apply simulated leading to create leading strips. Apply leading strips to window, following pattern. Paint surface with glass paint, using the Vertical Technique.

¼ of Entry Door Pattern   Enlarge 170%

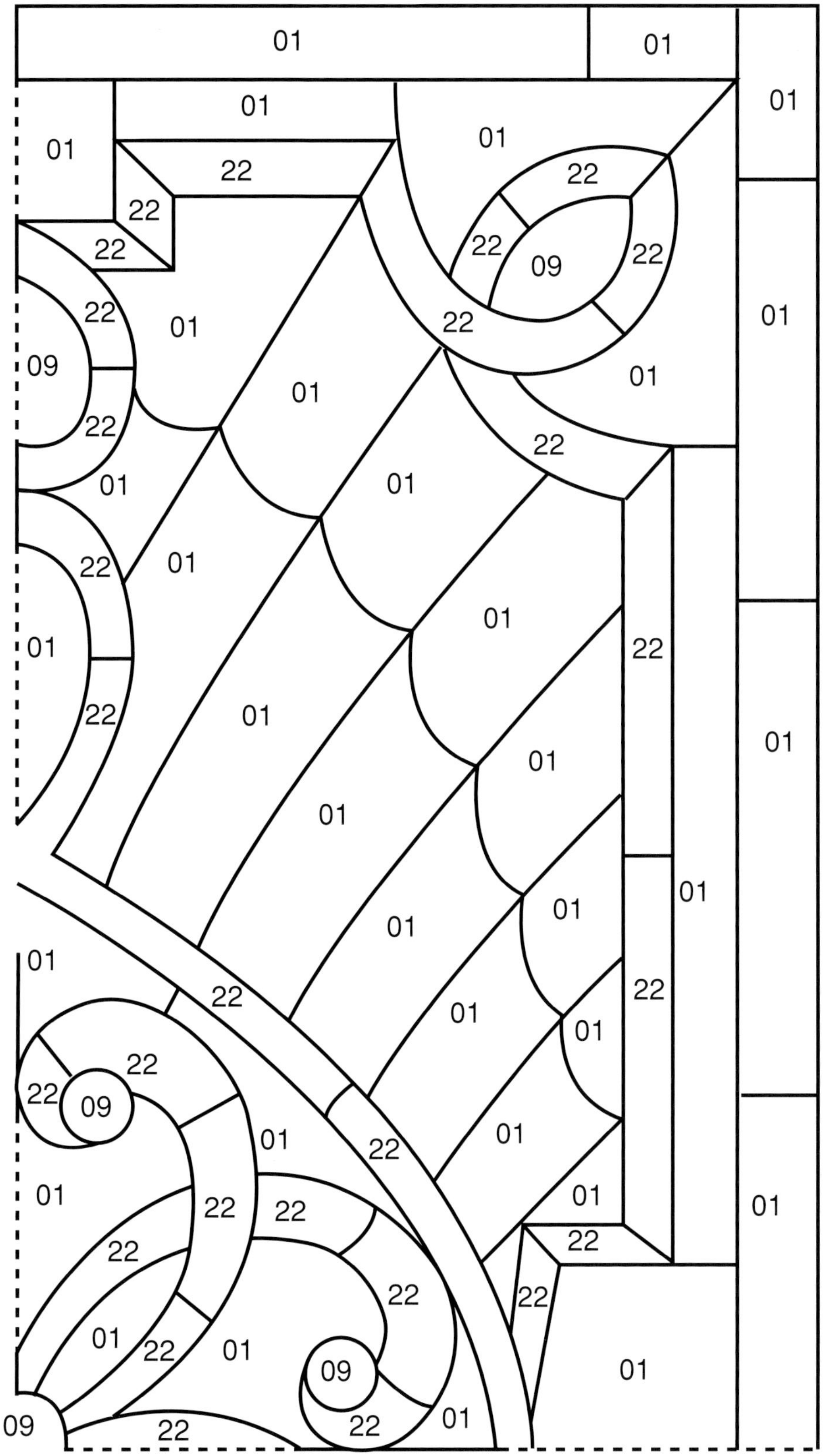

Horizontal Center Line

55

Sassy Suncatchers

They brighten your home, brighten your day, and brighten your spirits. A suncatcher captures the sunlight and passes it on in radiant color and design.

Suncatchers are flexible, transparent, removable window decorations that look like stained glass. They adhere to glass without any adhesive or hardware and can easily be peeled off for later use. The suncatcher projects in this book are so easy the entire family can participate in decorating your home.

How to Make Your Suncatcher

Using Leading Blanks

Suncatchers are leaded and painted on plastic. The best material is a leading blank.

1 Cover your work surface with a piece of white posterboard.

2 Lay your traced pattern on this surface and cover it with the leading blank. You will be able to see the pattern lines through the leading blank.

Using Plastic-Covered Cardboard

Plastic-covered cardboard is an alternative to a leading blank. Do not use hard plastics that resemble glass, as suncatchers will not peel up from them. Adhesion to these surfaces is permanent.

1 Tape your traced pattern to a piece of cardboard. Place a piece of non-clinging plastic (such as a drycleaning bag) over the design. Do not use kitchen plastic wrap.

2 Cover the entire sheet of cardboard with one piece of plastic. Tape the plastic down on the backside of the cardboard.

Leading the Suncatcher

1 Lead the pattern lines directly onto the leading blank or plastic-covered cardboard as you would for the Modular Technique of doing glass art projects. See "Leading the Design Using the Modular Technique" on page 19. Simply follow pattern lines with cords of simulated leading squeezed from the leading bottle.

2 Let the leading dry for at least eight hours before adding paint.

3 If you are working on a leading blank, use your fingernail after the leading is dry to pull up any unwanted leading and snip off or trim it away with small scissors. Lay the leading line that remains back on the leading blank and press firmly in place.

If using plastic-covered cardboard, remove unwanted leading from within the perimeter of the design, using a cotton swab. Leading that protrudes from the outer edge of the design can be cut off with scissors after the suncatcher is painted, cured, and peeled up.

Painting the Suncatcher

1 Paint the sections of the design with glass art paint. See "Painting the Design Using the

Modular Technique" on page 20. Add a generous amount of paint into each section, up to the top of the leading. (Do not add so much that it overflows the reservoir made by the leading.) If the colored area is too thin, it may tear when removed from the plastic. Also, comb and tap to evenly distribute paint and minimize bubbles as described in previous instructions for the Modular Technique.

2 Let the project dry for 24 to 48 hours on a dry, flat surface with good air circulation, such as the top of the refrigerator. Drying time may vary, depending on the thickness of the paint and the humidity. All cloudy areas must turn transparent before proceeding. After the suncatcher has dried, it can be removed from your base surface. Like magic, the painted and leaded design will peel up from your plastic. Place the suncatcher on a clean glass surface where it will "stick" until you wish to peel it off of the glass surface.

Applying & Removing the Suncatcher

Applying:
Place the suncatcher on a clean window or mirror. Smooth the design from the center outward to avoid air bubbles. Do not place suncatchers on moist windows. Colored moisture could run down the window and stain the sill.

Removing:
Lift the edge and pull gently. If it seems brittle or resists removal, warm it first by blowing air on it with a hair dryer. If the window becomes too warm, the suncatcher may stretch during removal. Wait for the window to cool before pulling it off.

Reusing:
If the suncatcher will not stick when reapplying, clean the back with a paper towel moistened with window cleaner before putting it on the window. Also, clean the window with window cleaner before application.

Storing:
Place the suncatchers on leading blanks, press out any air bubbles, and store in a plastic bag. Keep flat until ready to reapply. NEVER store any glass art paint project with paper or tissue around it. The paper fibers will adhere to the surface. If this should happen inadvertently, fibers can sometimes be worked out of the surface with a damp cloth.

TIPS:
- When designing your own suncatchers, limit the size to approximately 5" square for maximum durability.

- Make designs in segments so each color has a closed section. If using a design of your own or from another source, add lines to your design where needed before leading the design. Segmenting also helps achieve the look of genuine stained glass.

- Remove just one or a few painted sections that you wish to repaint. Wait until the paint is dry, remove the suncatcher from the leading blank or plastic, and use small scissors to cut the paint as close as possible to the leading line and remove it. Place the suncatcher on plastic again, press flat, and apply another color. Let the new color dry.

- Move the suncatcher to a location with the least moisture if a cloudy appearance remains when the suncatcher is dry. Cured suncatchers may look cloudy during display if there is excess moisture on the surface. NOTE: All glass art paints have a milky appearance immediately after application, but they will be clear when dry.

Summertime Suncatchers

GATHER THESE SUPPLIES

2 oz. Glass Paint for Bees:
03 = Cameo Ivory
07 = Cocoa Brown
20 = Amber

2 oz. Glass Paint for Beehive:
07 = Cocoa Brown
20 = Amber

2 oz. Glass Paint for Magenta Pot:
03 = Cameo Ivory
17 = Magenta Royal

2 oz. Glass Paint for Butterfly:
03 = Cameo Ivory
07 = Cocoa Brown
13 = Slate Blue
14 = Amethyst
24 = Ivy Green

2 oz. Glass Paint for Tulips:
03 = Cameo Ivory
06 = Canyon Coral
08 = Kelly Green

2 oz. Glass Paint for Watering Can:
02 = Snow White
04 = Sunny Yellow
09 = Emerald Green
12 = Royal Blue

INSTRUCTIONS

Prepare:
1. See "Patterns" on page 7. Prepare patterns.

Apply:
2. See "How to Make Your Suncatcher" on pages 56-57. Apply liquid leading and paint to leading blank or plastic-covered cardboard surface. Apply suncatcher to glass surface.

Pattern Actual Size

Pattern Actual Size

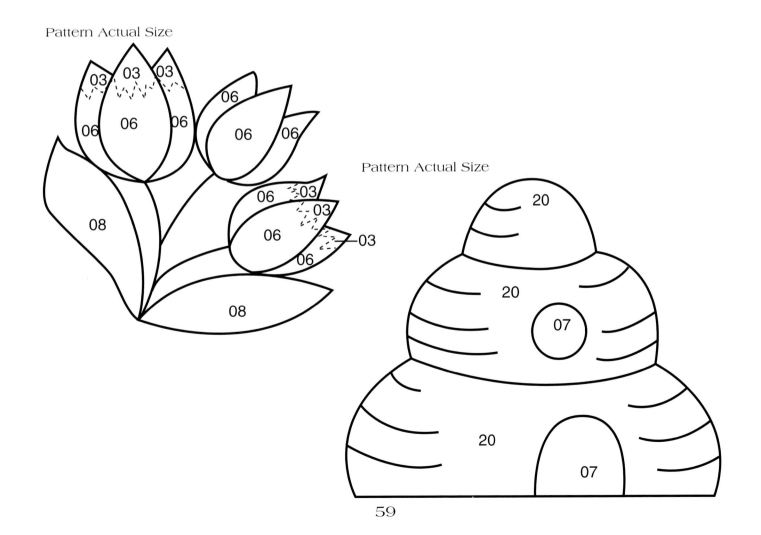

59

Pattern Actual Size   For denim pot, replace color 17 with color 10.

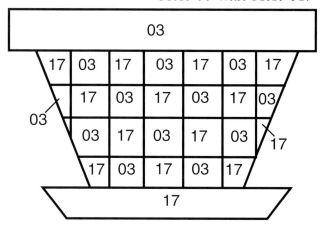

| 17 | 03 | 17 | 03 | 17 | 03 | 17 |
| | 17 | 03 | 17 | 03 | 17 | 03 |
03
| | 03 | 17 | 03 | 17 | 03 | 17 |
| | 17 | 03 | 17 | 03 | 17 | |

03

03   17

17

Pattern Actual Size

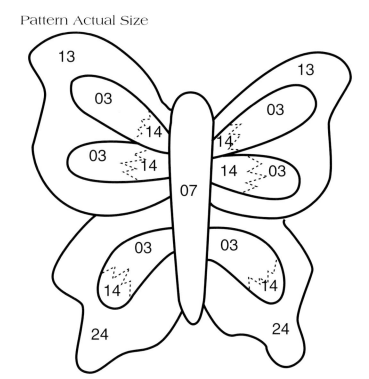

Pattern Actual Size

20   20

07
20
03   07   03
20
07
20

Pattern Actual Size

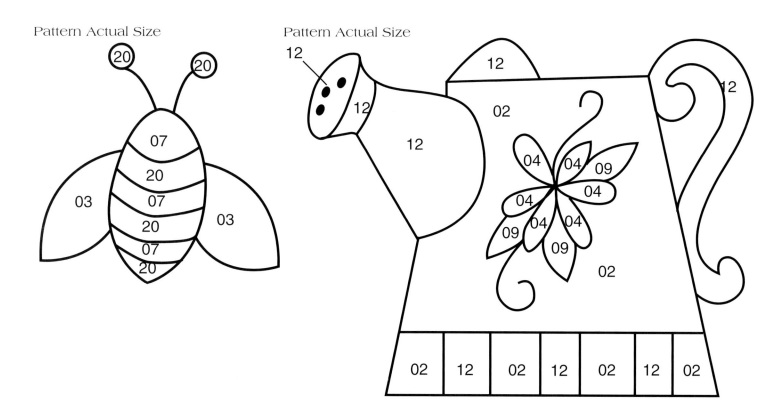

12

12

12   12

12   02

12

04   04   09
04
04   04
09   04   04
09

02

| 02 | 12 | 02 | 12 | 02 | 12 | 02 |

Autumn Suncatchers

Pictured on page 61.

GATHER THESE SUPPLIES

2 oz. Glass Paint for Acorns:
03 = Cameo Ivory
07 = Cocoa Brown

2 oz. Glass Paint for Nest Eggs:
07 = Cocoa Brown
10 = Denim Blue

2 oz. Glass Paint for Fruit Bowl:
02 = Snow White
07 = Cocoa Brown
10 = Denim Blue
20 = Amber
23 = Berry Red
24 = Ivy Green

2 oz. Glass Paint for Leaves:
04 = Sunny Yellow
05 = Orange Poppy
15 = Ruby Red

INSTRUCTIONS

Prepare:
1. See "Patterns" on page 7. Prepare patterns.

Apply:
2. See "How to Make Your Suncatcher" on pages 56-57. Apply simulated leading and paint to leading blank or plastic-covered cardboard surface. Apply suncatcher to glass surface.

Pattern Actual Size

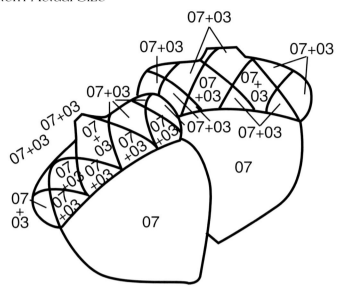

Pattern Actual Size

Pattern Actual Size

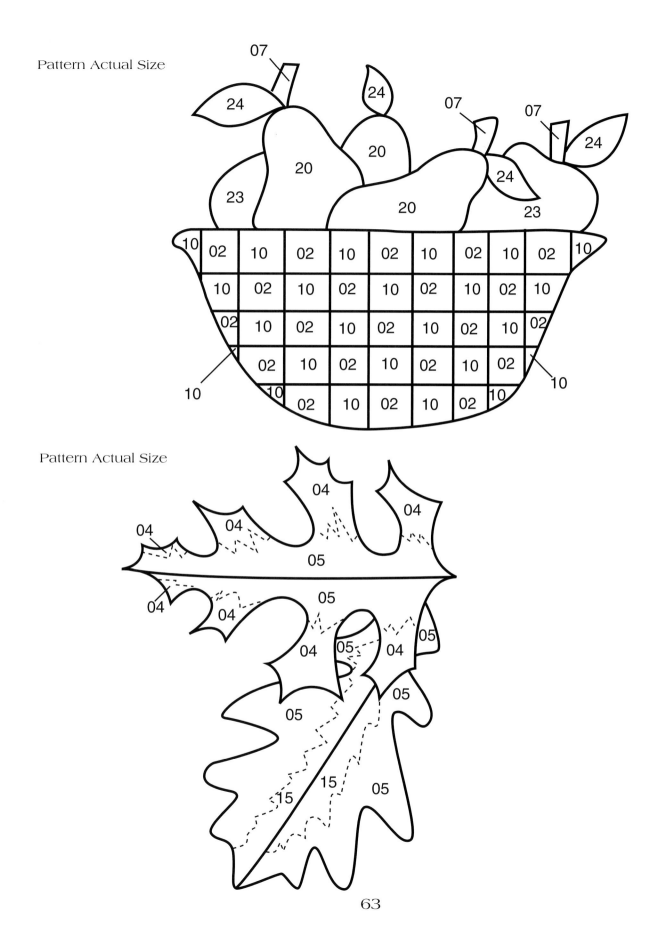

Pattern Actual Size

63

Home Scene Suncatchers

GATHER THESE SUPPLIES

2 oz. Glass Paint for Pitcher:
02 = Snow White
10 = Denim Blue
20 = Amber
23 = Berry Red
24 = Ivy Green

2 oz. Glass Paint for Brown Bird:
02 = Snow White
07 = Cocoa Brown
20 = Amber
23 = Berry Red

2 oz. Glass Paint for Birdhouse:
02 = Snow White
07 = Cocoa Brown
13 = Slate Blue
20 = Amber
23 = Berry Red

2 oz. Glass Paint for Cat:
02 = Snow White
06 = Canyon Coral
07 = Cocoa Brown
10 = Denim Blue

INSTRUCTIONS

Prepare:
1. See "Patterns" on page 7. Prepare patterns.

Apply:
2. See "How to Make Your Suncatcher" on pages 56-57. Apply simulated leading and paint to leading blank or plastic-covered cardboard surface. Apply suncatcher to glass surface.

Pattern Actual Size

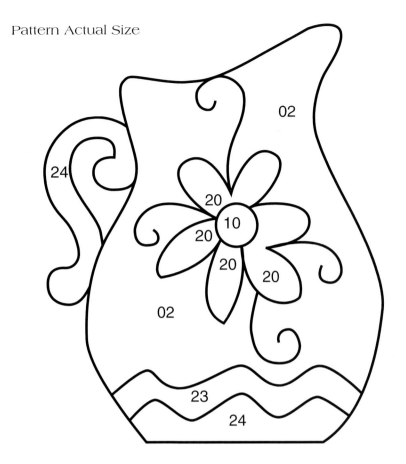

Pattern Actual Size

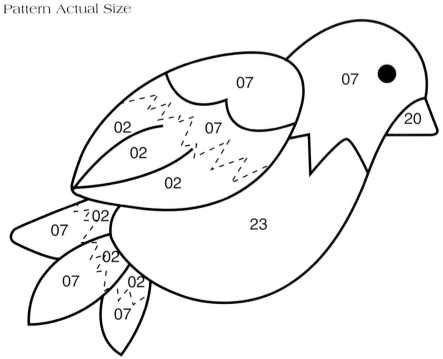

65

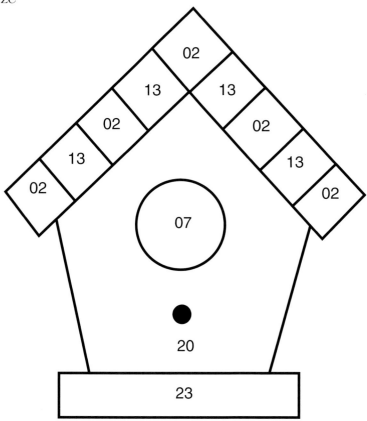

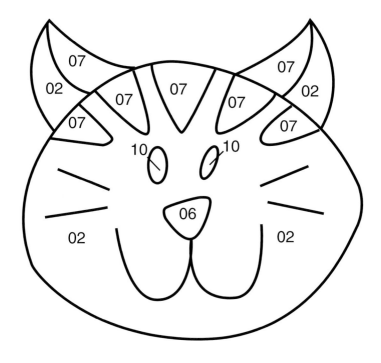

Spooky Halloween Suncatchers

Pictured on page 67.

GATHER THESE SUPPLIES

2 oz. Glass Paint for Yellow Bird:
03 = Cameo Ivory
18 = Charcoal Black
20 = Amber

2 oz. Glass Paint for Ghost:
02 = Snow White
04 = Sunny Yellow

05 = Orange Poppy
09 = Emerald Green
18 = Charcoal Black

2 oz. Glass Paint for Scarecrow:
02 = Snow White
04 = Sunny Yellow
05 = Orange Poppy
09 = Emerald Green
12 = Royal Blue
15 = Ruby Red

2 oz. Glass Paint for Pumpkin:
04 = Sunny Yellow
05 = Orange Poppy
09 = Emerald Green

INSTRUCTIONS

Prepare:
1. See "Patterns" on page 7. Prepare patterns.

Apply:
2. See "How to Make Your Suncatcher" on pages 56-57. Apply simulated leading and paint to leading blank or plastic-covered cardboard surface. Apply suncatcher to glass surface.

Pattern Actual Size

68

Enlarge 140%

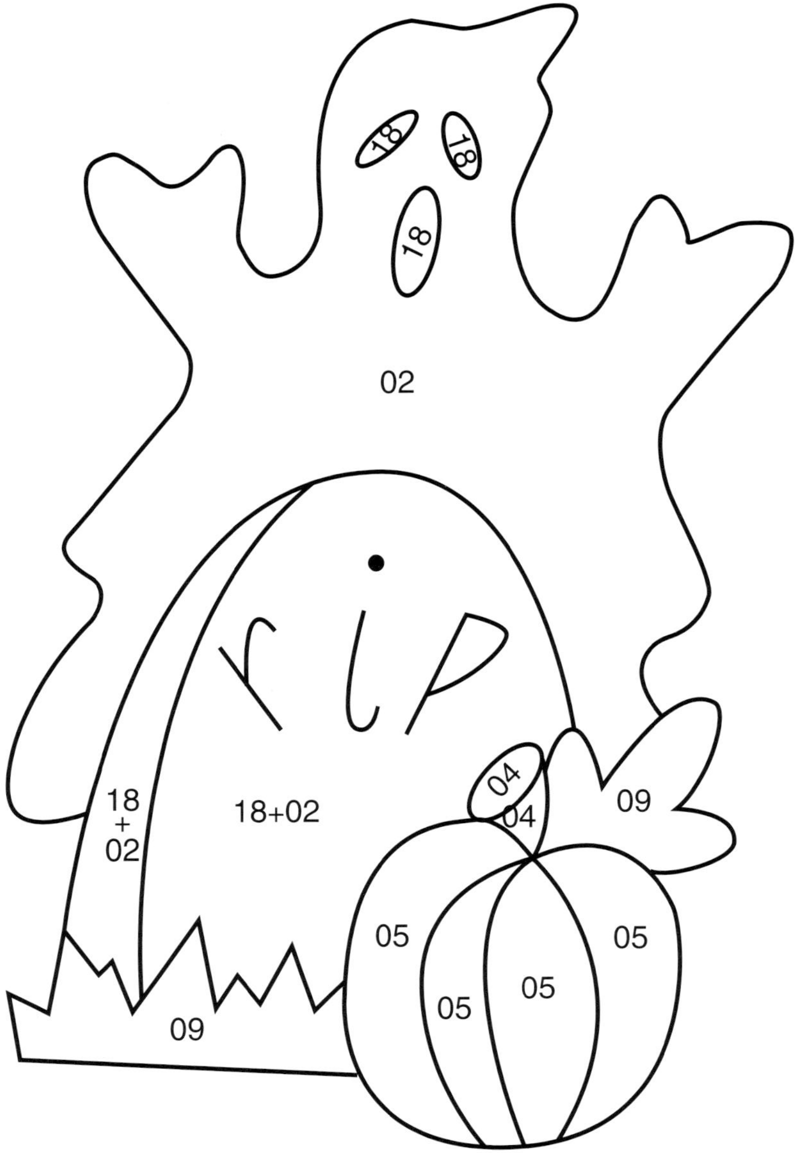
18
18
18
02
rip
18
+
02
18+02
04
04
09
05
05
05
05
09

Enlarge 200%

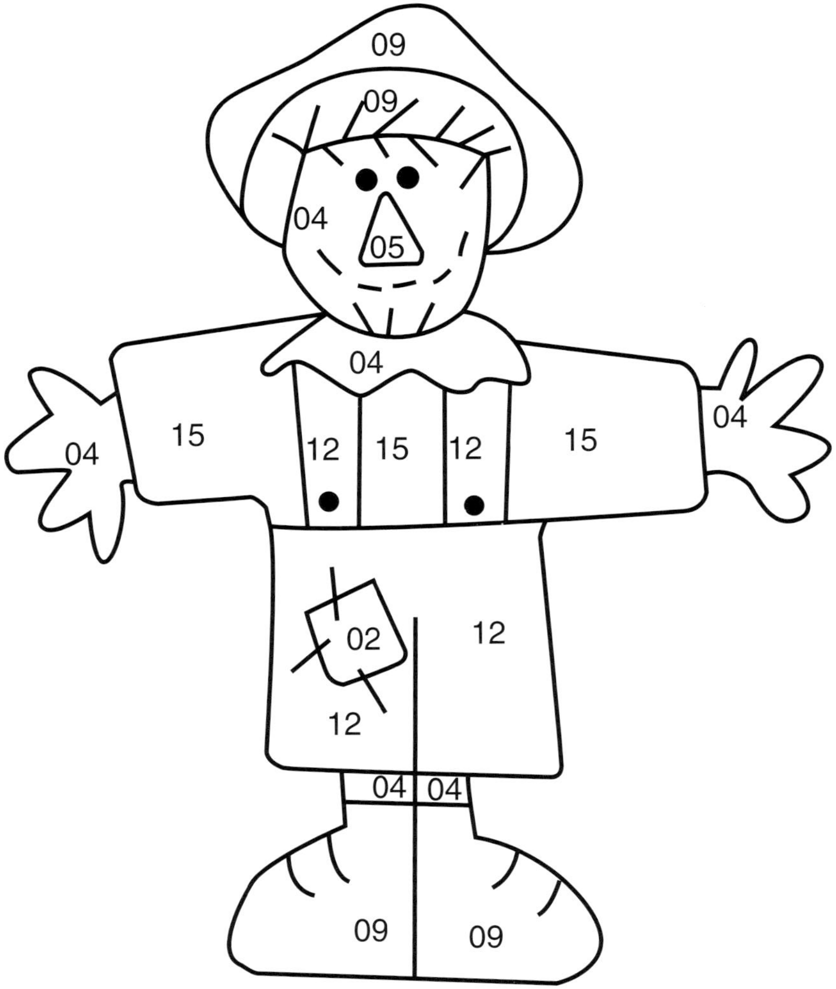
09
09
04
05
04
04
15
12
15
12
15
04
02
12
12
04
04
09
09

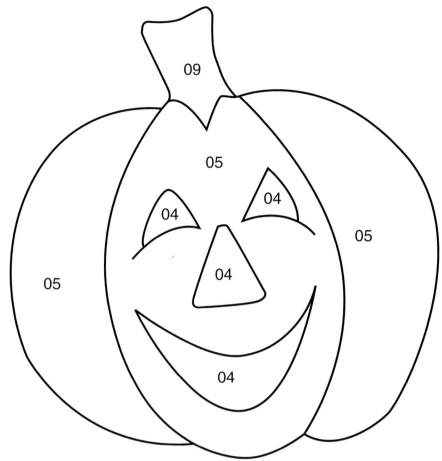

How to Make Window Scenes & Borders

Here are more unique ways to use glass art painted designs. An entire window scene can be created with a collection of suncatchers. These are not only wonderful for holiday decoration, but create an interesting effect for use throughout the year. Coordinate a scene with your home decor or create scenes which change with the seasons. Another way to use glass art window designs is with borders. This way you do not have to give up your view through the window. The many possibilities will include one that fits your needs.

Making Window Scenes

1 Make the individual suncatchers that you will need to create the scene. See "How to Make Your Suncatcher" on pages 56-57. Apply them to glass surface.

2 Add lines of simulated leading to connect them. If desired, paint in the background between leading lines, painting directly on the window.

Making Window Borders

1 Make the suncatcher that you will need to create the border. See "How to Make Your Suncatcher" on pages 56-57.

2 Place and adhere the suncatchers on the sides, across the top and/or bottom, on the sides, or in the corners.

Christmas Scene

Enlarge 135%

Pictured on page 71.

GATHER THESE SUPPLIES

2 oz. Glass Paint for Christmas Tree:
02 = Snow White
04 = Sunny Yellow
09 = Emerald Green

2 oz. Glass Paint for Gingerbread House:
02 = Snow White
04 = Sunny Yellow
05 = Orange Poppy
07 = Cocoa Brown
09 = Emerald Green
15 = Ruby Red

2 oz. Glass Paint for Gingerbread Boy & Girl:
02 = Snow White
07 = Cocoa Brown
09 = Emerald Green
15 = Ruby Red

INSTRUCTIONS

Prepare:
1. See "Patterns" on page 7. Prepare patterns.

Apply:
2. See "How to Make Window Scenes & Borders" on page 70. Make suncatchers. Apply suncatchers to glass surface to create scene.

Enlarge 135%

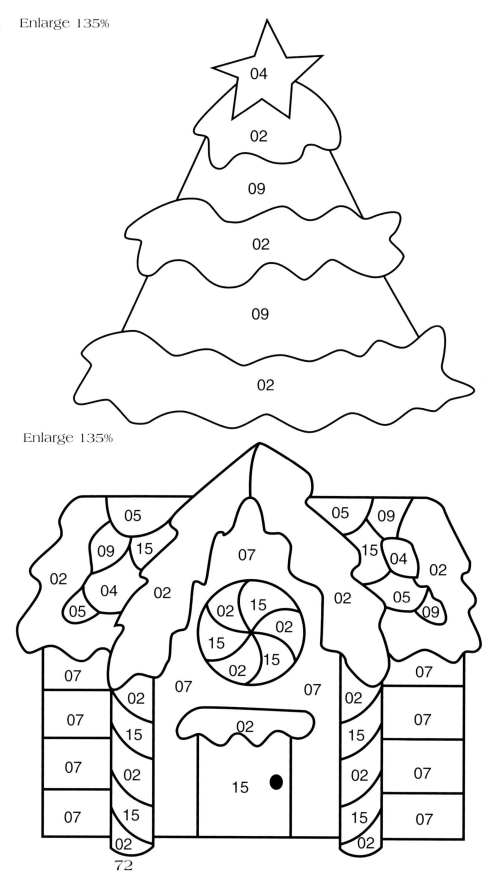

72

Merry Christmas Window

Bring holiday cheer to virtually any window, using these colorful ornaments. If your windows have existing mullions, or if you create your own with simulated leading, apply "snow drifts" at consistent angles. On a window with no divided panes, reverse the snow drifts in the two lower corners. For full-glass windows without mullions, you can drape a curved strand of simulated leading to "attach" your simulated leading ornament strings.

GATHER THESE SUPPLIES

Glass Stain Paint:
04 = Sunny Yellow
08 = Kelly Green
11 = Blue Diamond
12 = Royal Blue
14 = Amethyst
15 = Ruby Red
19 = Gold Sparkle
21 = White Pearl

INSTRUCTIONS

Prepare:
1. See "Patterns" on page 7. Prepare patterns.

Apply:
2. See "How to Make Window Scenes & Borders" on page 70. Make suncatchers. Apply suncatchers to glass surface to create scene.

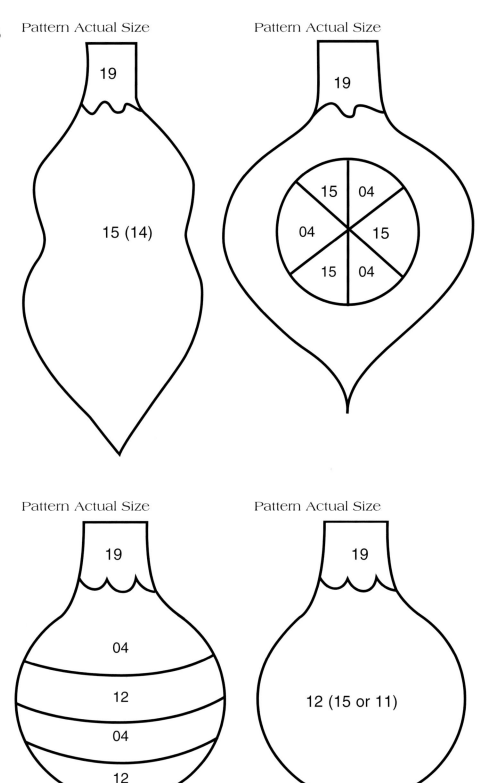

Pattern Actual Size

Pattern Actual Size

Pattern Actual Size

Pattern Actual Size

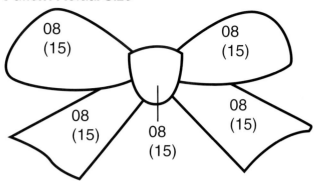

08
(15)

08
(15)

08
(15)

08
(15)

08
(15)

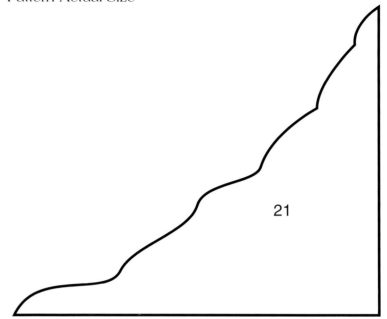

21

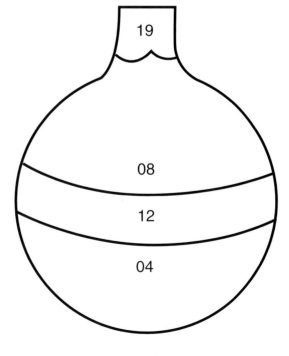

19

08

12

04

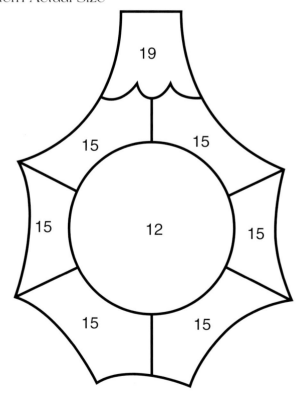

19

15

15

15

15

12

15

15

Roses, Roses Window

Pictured on page 77.

These "corner" designs are grouped to create a coordinating center design that goes on windows with or without divided panes. You may want to create just the center design or just the corners. For kitchens, color the roses with Sunny Yellow or Ruby Red for a brighter effect. Each variegated leaf was colored with three dots of Kelly Green swirled into Cameo Ivory.

GATHER THESE SUPPLIES

2 oz. Glass Paint:
03 = Cameo Ivory
08 = Kelly Green
16 = Rose Quartz

INSTRUCTIONS

Prepare:
1. See "Patterns" on page 7. Prepare patterns.

Apply:
2. See "How to Make Window Scenes & Borders" on page 70. Make suncatchers. Apply suncatchers to glass surface to create border.

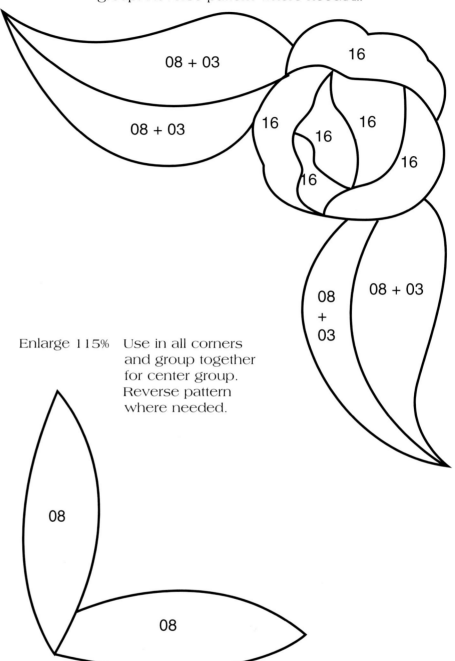

Enlarge 115%   Use in all corners and group together for center group. Reverse pattern where needed.

Enlarge 115%   Use in all corners and group together for center group. Reverse pattern where needed.

78

Colorful Columbine

Pictured on page 79.

This versatile design fits every application need. Adjust flowers and leaves as you wish. Or let your window determine how few or how many flowers you need, then let your imagination help you create the positioning for them.

GATHER THESE SUPPLIES

2 oz. Glass Paint:
04 = Sunny Yellow
08 = Kelly Green
11 = Blue Diamond
21 = Pearl White

INSTRUCTIONS

Prepare:
1. See "Patterns" on page 7. Prepare patterns.

Apply:
2. See "How to Make Window Scenes & Borders" on page 70. Make suncatchers. Apply suncatchers to glass surface to create border.

Enlarge 190%   Top Center

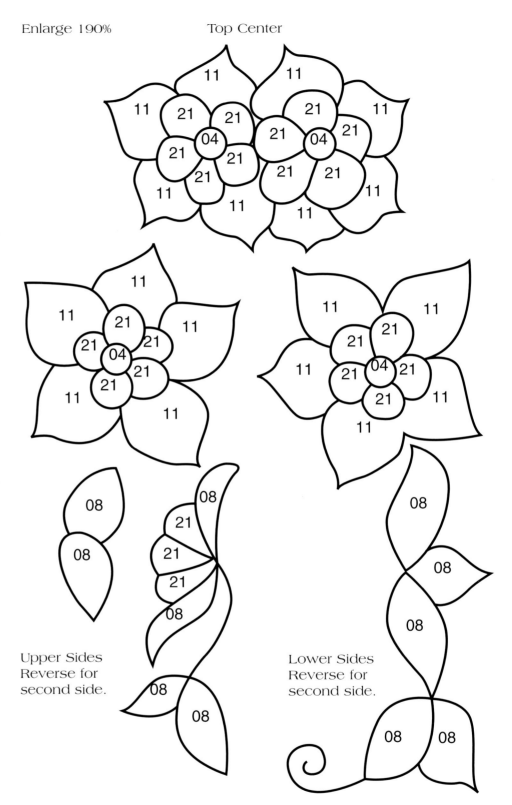

Upper Sides Reverse for second side.

Lower Sides Reverse for second side.

The All American Apple

Pictured on page 81.

There is no motif more cheerful than the apple! Repeat apples as many times as needed to go across window. Repeat checkered border above and below apples.

GATHER THESE SUPPLIES

2 oz. Glass Paints:
01 = Crystal Clear
02 = Snow White
07 = Cocoa Brown
08 = Kelly Green
12 = Royal Blue
15 = Ruby Red

INSTRUCTIONS

Prepare:
1. See "Patterns" on page 7. Prepare patterns.

Apply:
2. See "How to Make Window Scenes & Borders" on page 70. Make suncatchers. Apply suncatchers to glass surface to create border.

Enlarge 135%

Victorian Rose Border

Pictured on page 83.

The gentility and beauty of roses are captured in this lovely border. Match up pattern at dotted lines and repeat as needed to go across width of window.

GATHER THESE SUPPLIES

2 oz. Glass Paint:
01 = Crystal Clear
02 = Snow White
04 = Sunny Yellow
08 = Kelly Green
11 = Blue Diamond
16 = Rose Quartz
17 = Magenta Royal

INSTRUCTIONS

Prepare:
1. See "Patterns" on page 7. Prepare patterns.

Apply:
2. See "How to Make Window Scenes & Borders" on page 70. Make suncatchers. Apply suncatchers to glass surface to create border.

Enlarge 190%

84

Accessories for Home Decor

The versatility of glass art painting is never more evident than with the variety of home accessories you can make, including the decoration of three-dimensional glass items. These home decor accents, ranging from lamps to vases and more, will have the look of authentic (and often expensive) leaded glass found in boutiques.

Tiffany-Style Lamp

Light from a lamp is another way to illuminate glass art designs. Each glass panel of this lamp is removed from the lampshade, leaded, and painted flat. Panels are reassembled when dry.

GATHER THESE SUPPLIES

Lamp with glass lampshade

2 oz. Glass Paint:
03 = Cameo Ivory
04 = Sunny Yellow
10 = Denim Blue
12 = Royal Blue
13 = Slate Blue
14 = Amethyst
24 = Ivy Green

INSTRUCTIONS

Prepare:
1. See "Surface Preparation" on page 8. Prepare glass surface.

2. See "Patterns" on page 7. Prepare pattern.

Apply:
3. See "How to Use the Horizontal Technique" on page 17. Apply simulated leading and paint, using the Horizontal Technique.

Enlarge 155%

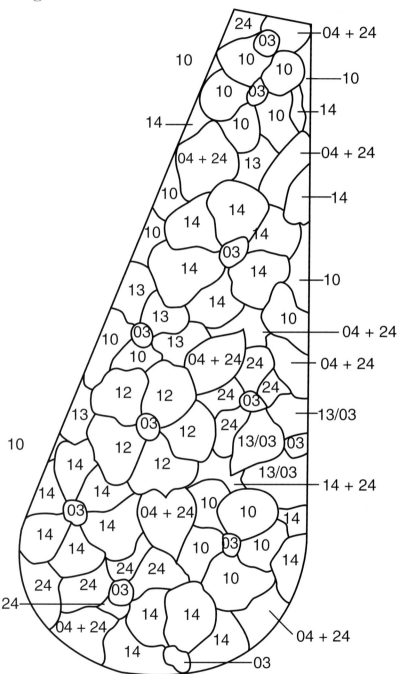

Night-Night Lights

GATHER THESE SUPPLIES

Night light with cool burning bulb

2 oz. Glass Paint for Floral Night Light:
17 = Magenta Royal
24 = Ivy Green

2 oz. Glass Paint for Teddy Bear Night Light:
03 = Cameo Ivory
07 = Cocoa Brown
12 = Royal Blue
18 = Charcoal Black

2 oz. Glass Paint for Noah's Ark Light:
02 = Snow White
03 = Cameo Ivory
04 = Sunny Yellow
07 = Cocoa Brown
08 = Kelly Green
12 = Royal Blue
15 = Ruby Red
17 = Magenta Royal

Other Supplies:
Fine grit sandpaper
Hot glue gun and glue sticks
Needlenose pliers
Styrene blank sheet

INSTRUCTIONS

1. Remove the protective plastic sheet from one side of the styrene blank sheet.

2. Measure and mark the styrene blank sheet into four equal squares. Score the sheet along one of these lines with a craft knife. Bend the panel evenly along the scored line as if trying to fold it in half. The sheet should pop along the scored line. You now have two equal pieces of styrene, each

with a marked line across the center.

3. Score along the marked line across the center of each piece and pop each piece in half as you did before. You now have four small styrene sheets. Use one per night light.

4. Position one of the small styrene sheets over the selected design. Patterns for designs are on pages 88-89. Trace the perimeter of the design onto the side of the styrene sheet without the protective plastic film. Retrace the perimeter line with a craft knife, applying a steady pressure. Using a knife, score perpendicular lines in the area outside the design, going from the outer edge of the design to the edge of the sheet. See Fig. 1.

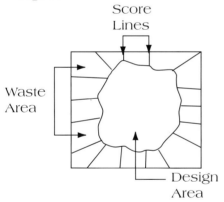

Fig. 1

5. Use needlenose pliers to "walk" around the perimeter of the design "biting" off little bits of styrene until you have taken away all excess styrene from around the design. Do not use force or your design will break. If you have little rough spots along the edge, carefully sand the edges with fine-grit

sandpaper. Avoid scratching the styrene surface.

6. Trace desired pattern lines on styrene shape.

Apply:
7. See "How to Use the Horizontal Technique" on page 17. Apply simulated leading and paint, using the Horizontal Technique. Let Dry.

8. Squeeze a pea-size spot of hot glue on the front in the area about half the distance between the bulb and the switch. See Fig. 2.

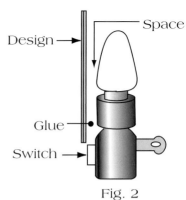

Fig. 2

9. Press the design piece onto the glue. Be careful not to lean the styrene surface against the bulb, or to cover the switch with the design.

Pattern Actual Size   Comb paint in direction of arrows.

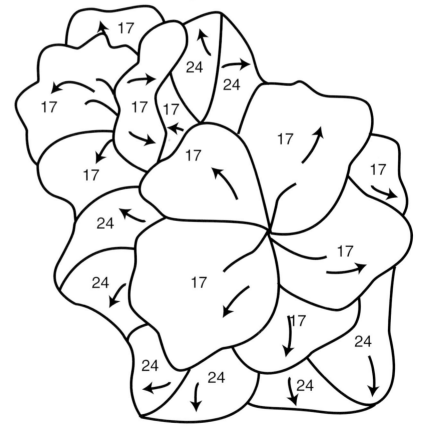

Pattern Actual Size

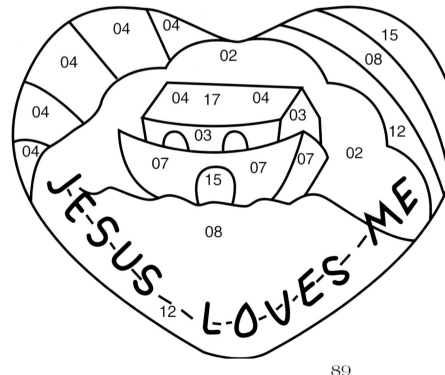

Nite - Nite

12
07
18 18
18
12
12
03
12
07
07
07
07
07
03
07
03
07
07
03

Pattern Actual Size

04 04
04 15
04 02 08
04 04 17 04 03
04 03 12
07 03 07 07 02
15
08
JE-S-US-L-O-V-E-S-ME
12

Pretty Plates for Display

Pictured on page 90.

GATHER THESE SUPPLIES

Glass plate(s)

2 oz. Glass Paint for Rose Plate:
03 = Cameo Ivory
16 = Rose Quartz
23 = Berry Red
24 = Ivy Green

2 oz. Glass Paint for Fruit Plate:
04 = Sunny Yellow
06 = Canyon Coral
07 = Cocoa Brown
08 = Kelly Green
14 = Amethyst
15 = Ruby Red
17 = Magenta Royal
20 = Amber
23 = Berry Red
24 = Ivy Green

INSTRUCTIONS

Prepare:
1. See "Surface Preparation" on page 8. Prepare glass surface.

2. See "Patterns" on page 7. Prepare and apply pattern to glass surface.

Apply:
3. See "How to Use the Horizontal Technique" on page 17. Apply simulated leading and paint, using the Horizontal Technique.

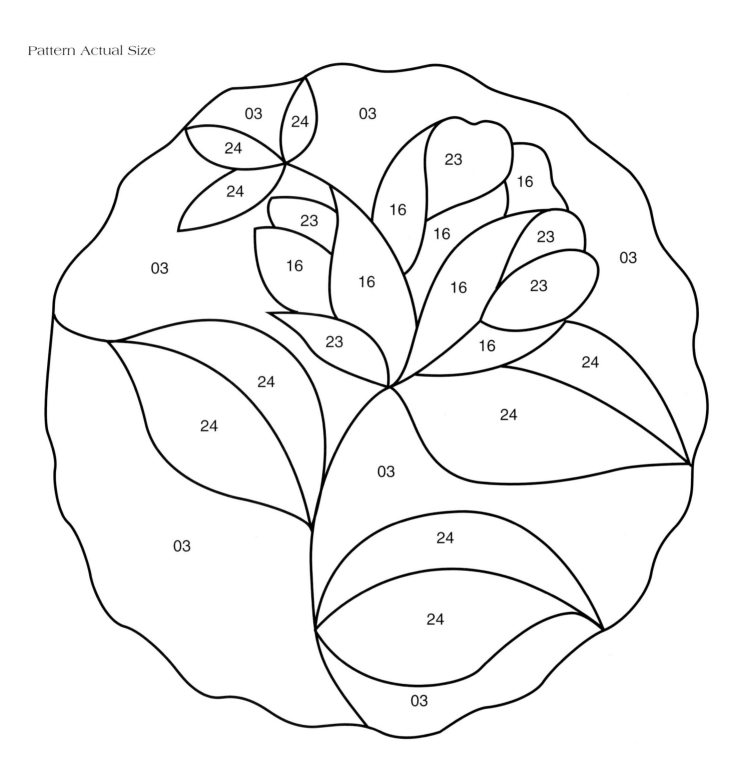

Teacher's Treats

Pictured on page 93.

GATHER THESE SUPPLIES

Glass Jar with lid

2 oz. Glass Paint:
02 = Snow White
15 = Ruby Red
20 = Amber
24 = Ivy Green

INSTRUCTIONS

Prepare:
1. See "Patterns" on page 7. Prepare patterns.

Apply:
2. See "Small Glass Art Projects" on pages 18-20. Apply simulated leading and paint to leading blank or plastic-covered cardboard, using the Modular Technique. Apply design to glass surface.

Pattern Actual Size

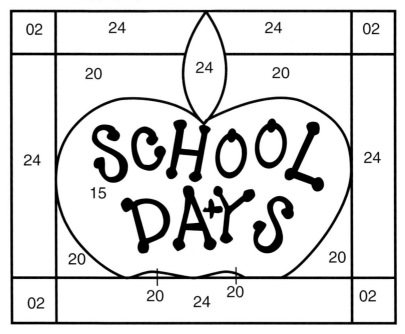

Pattern Actual Size

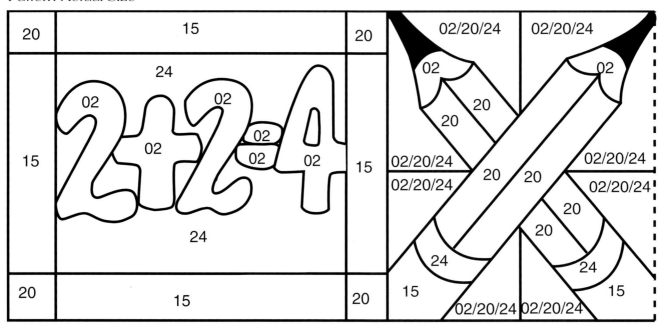

Candy Canister

Pictured on page 93.

GATHER THESE SUPPLIES

Glass jar with lid

2 oz. Glass Paint:
02 = Snow White
09 = Emerald Green
10 = Denim Blue
23 = Berry Red

INSTRUCTIONS

Prepare:
1. See "Patterns" on page 7. Prepare patterns.

Apply:
2. See "Small Glass Art Projects" on pages 18-20. Apply simulated leading and paint to leading blank or plastic-covered cardboard, using the Modular Technique. Apply design to glass surface.

Enlarge 150%   Repeat with second colors given in ( ).

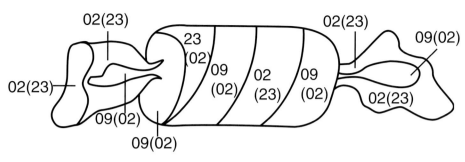

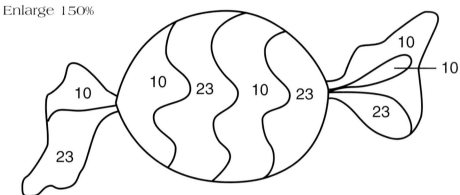

Enlarge 150%

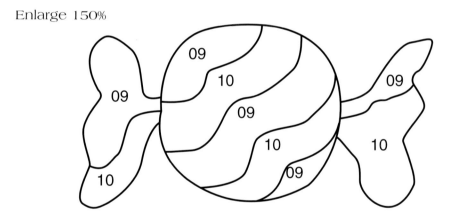

Enlarge 150%

Enlarge 150%

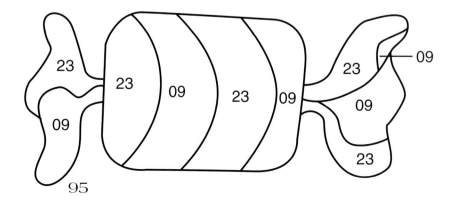

95

Trick or Treat Jar

Pictured on page 93.

GATHER THESE SUPPLIES

Glass jar with wooden lid

2 oz. Glass Paint:
02 = Snow White
04 = Sunny Yellow
05 = Orange Poppy
07 = Cocoa Brown
08 = Kelly Green
13 = Slate Blue

Other Supplies:
Acrylic paint: orange, white
Paint pen: black
Paintbrushes: flat; sponge
Varnish

INSTRUCTIONS

Prepare:
1. See "Patterns" on page 7. Prepare pattern.

Apply:
2. See "Small Glass Art Projects" on pages 18-20. Apply simulated leading and paint to leading blank or plastic-covered cardboard, using the Modular Technique. Apply design to glass surface.

3. Paint wooden lid with orange acrylic paint, using flat paintbrush. Let dry. Sponge wooden lid with white acrylic paint, using sponge paintbrush.

4. Place desired lettering on wooden lid with black pen.

5. Varnish wooden lid.

Pattern Actual Size

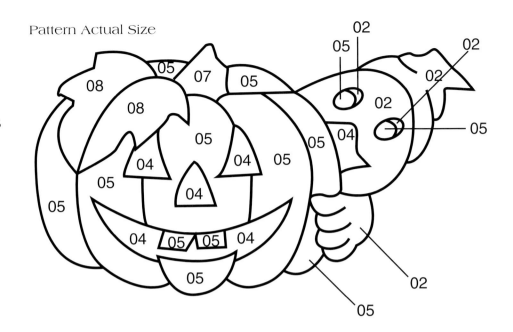

Pattern Actual Size

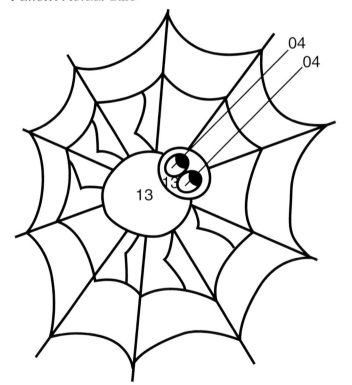

Sugar Canister

Pictured on page 93.

GATHER THESE SUPPLIES

Glass jar with lid

2 oz. Glass Paint:
19 = Gold Sparkle
24 = Ivy Green

INSTRUCTIONS

Prepare:
1. See "Surface Preparation" on page 8. Prepare glass surface.

2. See "Patterns" on page 7. Prepare patterns.

Apply:
3. See "How to Use the Horizontal Technique" on page 17. Apply liquid leading and paint, using the Horizontal Technique.

Pattern Actual Size

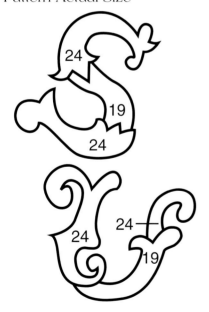

Pattern Actual Size

Star Votive

Pictured on page 98.

GATHER THESE SUPPLIES

Candle votive with candle

2 oz. Glass Paint:
01 = Crystal Clear (background)
19 = Gold Sparkle

INSTRUCTIONS

Prepare:
1. See "Surface Preparation" on page 8. Prepare glass surface.

2. See "Patterns" on page 7. Prepare pattern.

Apply:
3. See "How to Use the Horizontal Technique" on page 17. Apply simulated leading and paint, using the Horizontal Technique.

Enlarge 125%

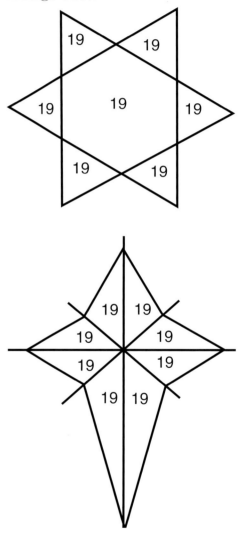

Rose Hurricane Lamp

Pattern Actual Size

Background color 01. Make two designs—one for each side of hurricane. Comb paint in direction of arrows.

NOTE: Rose Hurricane Lamp is for display only. The glass hurricane shade gets too hot for glass art paint when lit. Before using glass art paint on any glass hurricane shade or glass candleholder, test the glass for extreme heat. If the glass becomes too hot to the touch when a candle is lit, it is too hot for glass art paint.

GATHER THESE SUPPLIES

Glass hurricane

2 oz. Glass Paint:
01 = Crystal Clear
16 = Rose Quartz
24 = Ivy Green

INSTRUCTIONS

Prepare:
1. See "Patterns" on page 7. Prepare pattern.

Apply:
2. See "Small Glass Art Projects" on pages 18-20. Apply simulated leading and paint to leading blank or plastic-covered cardboard, using the Modular Technique. Apply design to glass surface.

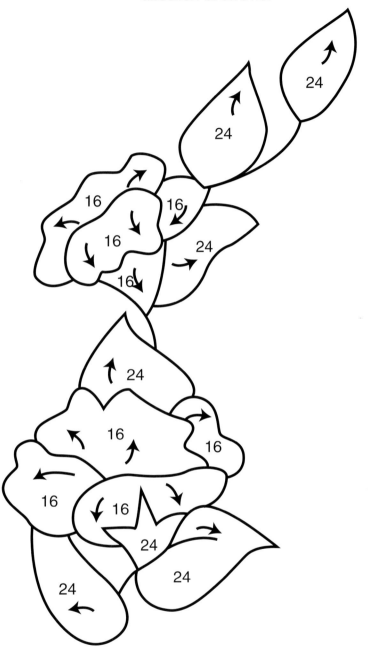

Pansy Candle

Pictured on page 98.

GATHER THESE SUPPLIES

Pillar candle: white

2 oz. Glass Paint:
02 = Snow White
03 = Cameo Ivory
11 = Blue Diamond
14 = Amethyst
17 = Magenta Royal
24 = Ivy Green

Other Supplies:
Wax: silver metallic

INSTRUCTIONS

Prepare:
1. See "Patterns" on page 7. Prepare pattern.

Apply:
2. See "Small Glass Art Projects" on pages 18-20. Apply simulated leading and paint to leading blank or plastic-covered cardboard, using the Modular Technique. Apply design to glass surface.

3. Coat bottom half of candle with silver metallic wax.

Pattern Actual Size

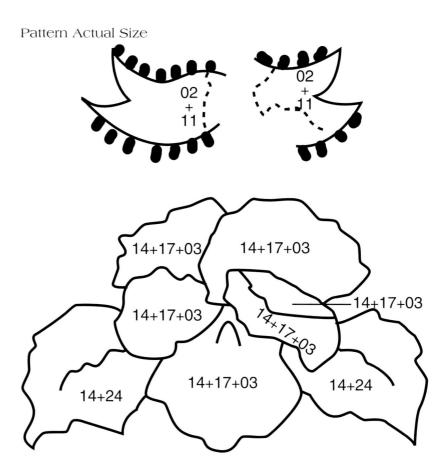

Fruit Slice Votive Candleholder

Pictured on page 98.

NOTE: Fruit Slice Votive Candleholder is for display only. The candleholder gets too hot for glass art paint when lit. Before using glass art paint on any glass hurricane shade or glass candleholder, test the glass for extreme heat. If the glass becomes too hot to the

Pattern Actual Size

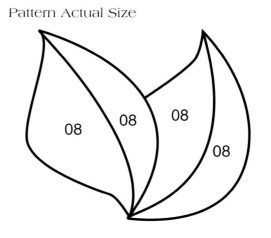

touch when a candle is in use, it is too hot for glass art paint.

GATHER THESE SUPPLIES

Glass candleholder

2 oz. Glass Paint:
02 = Snow White
04 = Sunny Yellow
05 = Orange Poppy
08 = Kelly Green

INSTRUCTIONS

Prepare:
1. See "Patterns" on page 7. Prepare patterns.

Apply:
2. See "Small Glass Art Projects" on pages 18-20. Apply simulated leading and paint to leading blank or plastic-covered cardboard, using the Modular Technique. Apply design to glass surface.

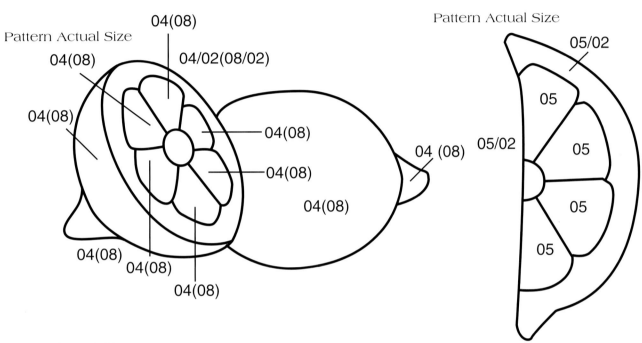

Pattern Actual Size

04(08)
04(08)
04/02(08/02)
04(08)
04(08)
04(08)
04(08)
04(08)
04(08)
04(08)
04 (08)

Pattern Actual Size

05/02
05
05/02
05
05
05

Pattern Actual Size

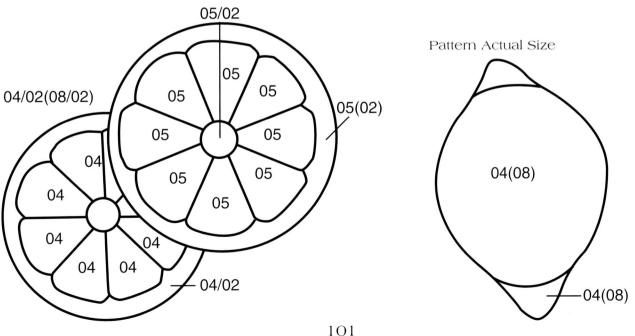

05/02
04/02(08/02)
05
05
05
05
05
05
05
05(02)
04
04
04
04
04
04
04/02

Pattern Actual Size

04(08)
04(08)

101

Large Floral Canister Jar

GATHER THESE SUPPLIES

Glass canister with lid

2 oz. Glass Paint:
02 = Snow White
23 = Berry Red
24 = Ivy Green

INSTRUCTIONS

Prepare:
1. See "Patterns" on page 7. Prepare pattern.

Apply:
2. See "Small Glass Art Projects" on pages 18-20. Apply simulated leading and paint to leading blank or plastic-covered cardboard, using the Modular Technique. Apply design to glass surface.

Enlarge 115%   Comb in direction of arrows.

103

Picked Cherries

Pictured on page 102.

GATHER THESE SUPPLIES

Glass jar with lid

2 oz. Glass Paint:
17 = Magenta Royal
24 = Ivy Green

INSTRUCTIONS

Prepare:
1. See "Patterns" on page 7. Prepare patterns.

Apply:
2. See "Small Glass Art Projects" on pages 18-20. Apply simulated leading and paint to leading blank or plastic-covered cardboard, using the Modular Technique. Apply design to glass surface.

Pattern Actual Size   Comb in direction of arrows.

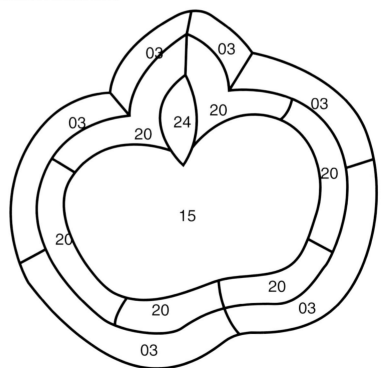

Apple Bottle

Pictured on page 102.

GATHER THESE SUPPLIES

Glass jar with lid

2 oz. Glass Paint:
03 = Cameo Ivory
15 = Ruby Red
20 = Amber
24 = Ivy green

INSTRUCTIONS

Prepare:
1. See "Patterns" on page 7. Prepare patterns.

Apply:
2. See "Small Glass Art Projects" on pages 18-20. Apply simulated leading and paint to leading blank or plastic-covered cardboard, using the Modular Technique. Apply design to glass surface.

Pattern Actual Size

Button Jar

Pictured on page 102.

GATHER THESE SUPPLIES

Glass jar with lid

2 oz. Glass Paint:
03 = Cameo Ivory
07 = Cocoa Brown
15 = Ruby Red
24 = Ivy Green

INSTRUCTIONS

Prepare:
1. See "Patterns" on page 7. Prepare patterns.

Apply:
2. See "Small Glass Art Projects" on pages 18-20. Apply simulated leading and paint to button cluster and pincushion, using the Modular Technique. Apply simulated leading and paint to needle and thread, using the Horizontal Technique. See "How to Use the Horizontal Technique" on page 17.

Pattern Actual Size   Divide top of jar with leading lines at corners. Paint two sides with color 15, alternating with two sides of color 24.

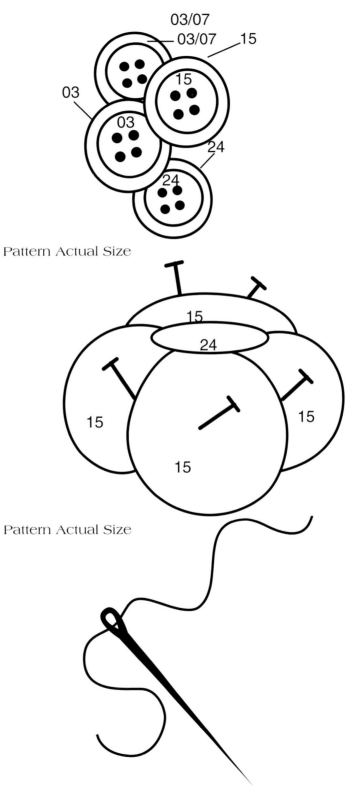

Pattern Actual Size

Pattern Actual Size

Pumpkin Seeds Jar

Pictured on page 102.

GATHER THESE SUPPLIES

Glass jar with lid

2 oz. Glass Paint:
04 = Sunny Yellow
05 = Orange Poppy
07 = Cocoa Brown
08 = Kelly Green

INSTRUCTIONS

Prepare:
1. See "Patterns" on page 7. Prepare patterns.

Apply:
2. See "Small Glass Art Projects" on pages 18-20. Apply simulated leading and paint to leading blank or plastic-covered cardboard, using the Modular Technique. Apply design to glass surface.

Pattern Actual Size   Divide jar outside modular design area with precured leading strips and paint sections with various solid colors.

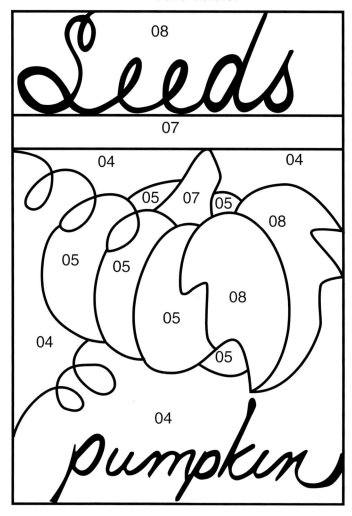

Iris Flower Vase

Pictured on page 107.

GATHER THESE SUPPLIES

Glass cylinder

2 oz. Glass Paint:
08 = Kelly Green
11 = Blue Diamond
20 = Amber
22 = Clear Frost

INSTRUCTIONS

Prepare:
1. See "Patterns" on page 7. Prepare pattern.

Apply:
2. See "Small Glass Art Projects" on pages 18-20. Apply simulated leading and paint to leading blank or plastic-covered cardboard, using the Modular Technique. Apply design to glass surface.

Iris Cylinder Vase

Pictured on page 107.

GATHER THESE SUPPLIES

Glass cylinder

2 oz. Glass Paint:
01 = Crystal Clear
04 = Sunny Yellow
08 = Kelly Green
14 = Amethyst
16 = Rose Quartz
17 = Magenta Royal

INSTRUCTIONS

Prepare:
1. See "Patterns" on page 7. Prepare pattern.

Apply:
2. See "Small Glass Art Projects" on pages 18-20. Apply simulated leading and paint to leading blank or plastic-covered cardboard, using the Modular Technique. Apply design to glass surface.

Tulip Cylinder Vase

Pictured on page 107.

GATHER THESE SUPPLIES

Glass cylinder

2 oz. Glass Paint:
01 = Crystal Clear
02 = Snow White
04 = Sunny Yellow
05 = Orange Poppy
08 = Kelly Green
15 = Ruby Red
17 = Magenta Royal

INSTRUCTIONS

Prepare:
1. See "Patterns" on page 7. Prepare pattern.

Apply:
2. See "Small Glass Art Projects" on pages 18-20. Apply simulated leading and paint to leading blank or plastic-covered cardboard, using the Modular Technique. Apply design to glass surface.

Pattern Actual Size Background color 22. Comb in direction of arrows. Repeat design as needed.

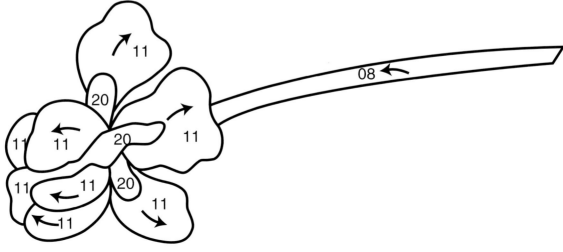

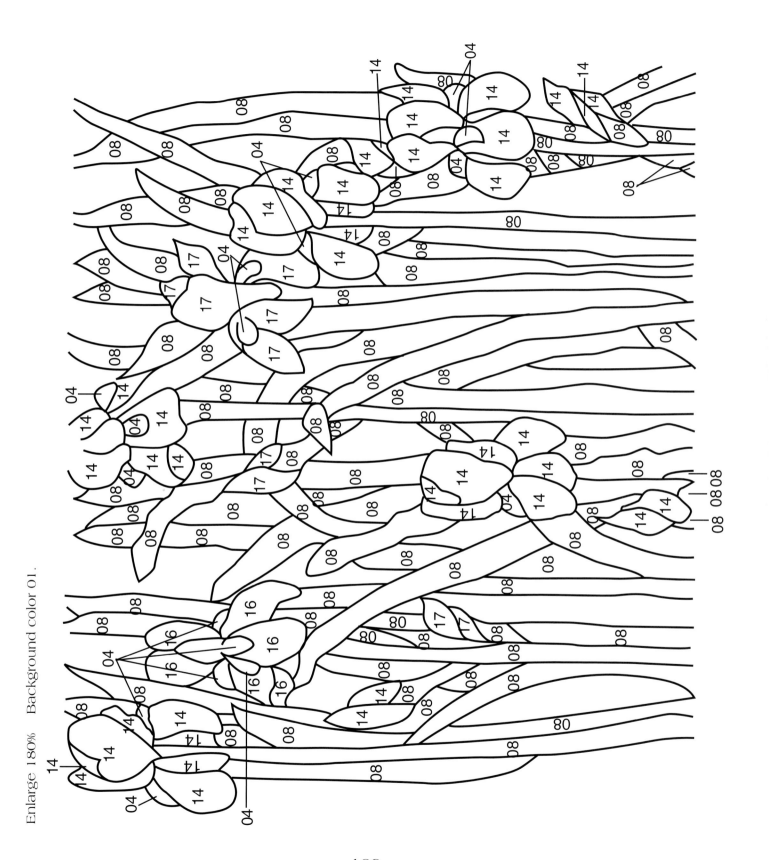

Enlarge 180%   Background color 01.

109

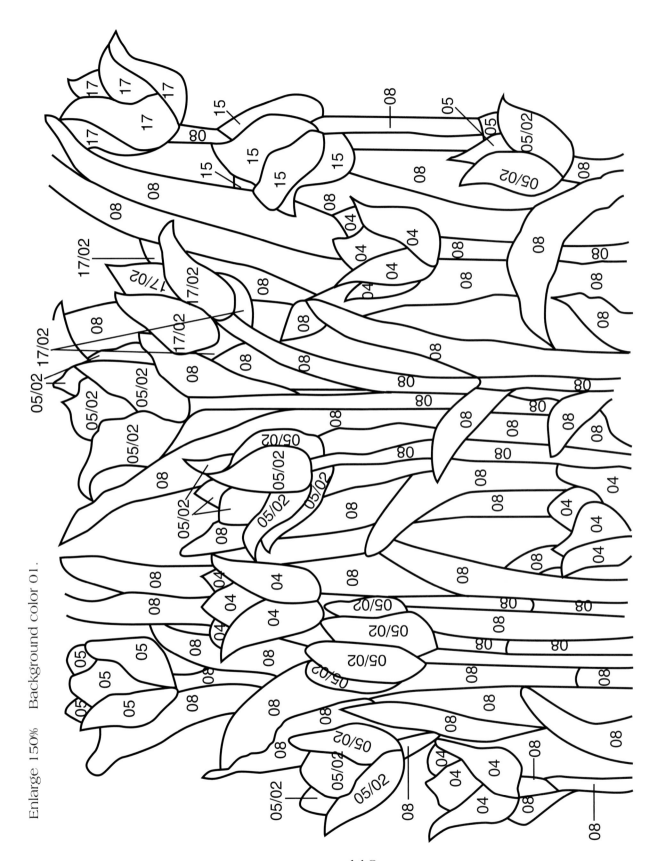

Enlarge 150%   Background color 01.

Ivy Cake Holder, Ivy Votive Candleholder, & Ivy Candleholder

Pictured on page 111.

Simple ivy makes a wonderfully warm design. For variegated Ivy Votive Candleholder, use two 2-leaf units and 1 single leaf. Do not connect with stems. On Ivy Cake Holder and Ivy Votive Candleholder, add leading lines for stems between leaves, using the Horizontal Method. See "Using the Horizontal Technique" on page 17. To make variegated ivy, apply Kelly Green to ¾ of each leaf toward the stem and apply Cameo Ivory to leaf tips.

GATHER THESE SUPPLIES

Glass cake holder
Glass candleholder
Glass votive candleholder

2 oz. Glass Paint for Ivy Cake Holder:
03 = Cameo Ivory
08 = Kelly Green

2 oz. Glass Paint for Ivy Votive Candleholder:
03 = Cameo Ivory
08 = Kelly Green

2 oz. Glass Paint for Ivy Candleholder:
22 = Clear Frost (Vertical Technique)
24 = Ivy Green

INSTRUCTIONS

Prepare:
1. See "Patterns" on page 7. Prepare patterns.

Apply:
2. See "Small Glass Art Projects" on pages 18-20.

Apply simulated leading and paint to leading blank or plastic-covered cardboard, using the Modular Technique. Apply design to glass surface.

.

Pattern Actual Size

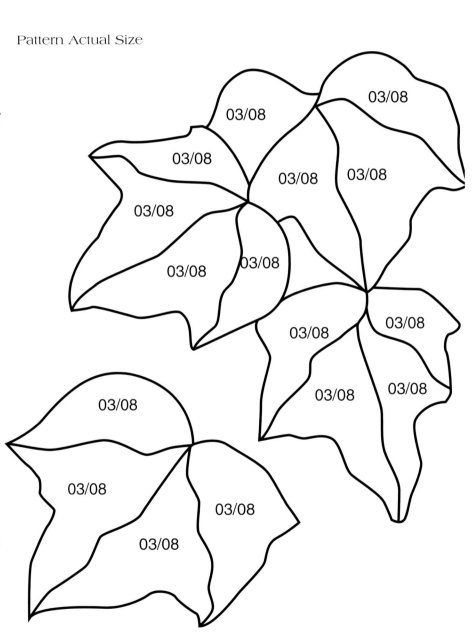

Flowers Around the Clock

Pictured on page 114.

GATHER THESE SUPPLIES

Mechanical clock

2 oz. Glass Paint:
08 = Kelly Green
13 = Slate Blue
17 = Magenta Royal
19 = Gold Sparkle

INSTRUCTIONS

Prepare:
1. See "Patterns" on page 7. Prepare patterns.

Apply:
2. See "Small Glass Art Projects" on pages 18-20. Apply simulated leading and paint to leading blank or plastic-covered cardboard, using the Modular Technique. Apply design to glass surface.

Enlarge 160% Background color 22.

Enlarge 150%   Comb paint in direction of arrows. Place heart at 12:00 position. When replacing clock parts, turn printed/numbered side of face to inside for a solid background.

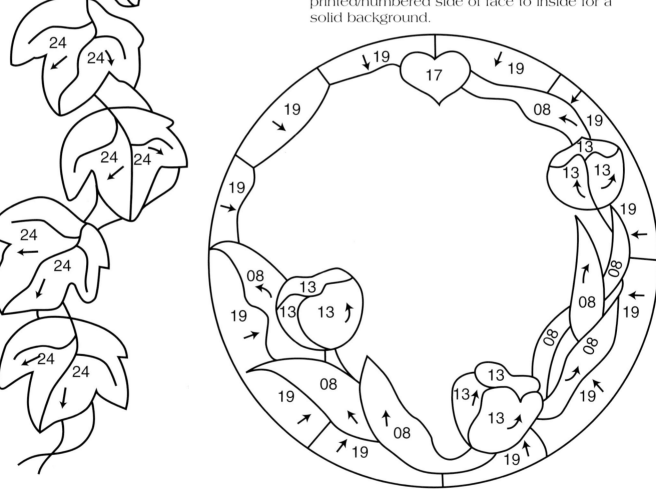

Desktop Delights

The following projects are wonderful to make for gifts or to use on entry tables, end tables, or for your own desk. Photo frames, candle windows, and privacy screens are fun and easy to make. Follow these same general instructions for creating the photo frames, candle windows, or privacy screens.

SUPPLIES YOU WILL NEED

Translucent Textured Glass Art Paint:
See "Translucent Textured Glass Art Paint" on page 6.

Simulated Leading:
See "Simulated Leading" on pages 6-7.

Design Blanks:
There are precut shapes available for creating table-top glass projects: a 3-Panel Screen, a Frame, and a Candle Window. These blank panels are of heavy plastic, a perfect surface for painting with glass paint. If these are not available, you can have thick, clear thermoplastic or styrene cut to the sizes as shown on the full-size design patterns.

Patterns:
See "Patterns" on page 7. The patterns given in this chapter are full-size patterns. To use, place the precut blank shape directly over pattern in book and lead design with simulated leading, following pattern lines. Apply paint colors as suggested or decide your own color scheme.

Other Supplies:
- Craft knife — for trimming leading
- Cotton swabs — for cleaning up paint that gets on leading
- Glass cleaner — for cleaning surfaces before leading is applied
- Masking tape — for taping blank plastic to pattern to keep blank from shifting while leading design
- Newspaper — for protecting work area
- Scissors — for trimming leading and cutting out traced patterns
- Toothpicks or nutpick — for combing out bubbles in paint
- Paper towels — for drying plastic blanks and wiping bottle tips and fingers
- Razor blade — for correcting mistakes
- Tracing paper — for tracing leading on blank

How to Create Glass Art Designs

Using Glass Art Paint

TIPS:
- Do not use outdoors or on surfaces in unregulated environments, such as storm doors, automobiles, and motor homes.

- Avoid using on surfaces that are in frequent contact with water or heavy condensation.

- Do not use on surfaces that are lower than 45° F or above 90° F during application or removal. (Extreme temperatures may cause cracking and/or distortion.)

- Practice to achieve consistent speed and pressure before beginning a project. Uneven lead lines indicate inconsistent speed when moving your arm. Bumps at the beginning or end of a line indicate too much pressure.

- Eliminate light holes in corners of painted sections by dabbing holes with liquid leading.

Displaying Your Frame

The opening on the pattern is for the inclusion of a photo. Cut a photo (or a color photo copy of a photo) so it is the exact measurement of the window opening. Using transparent tape, tape photo in place on back of painted project. The lead lines should be thick enough to hide the tape. Place in the wooden stand that is included with the Gallery Glass® Frame Blank or display on a small easel.

Displaying Your Candle Window

Display your candle window by placing it in the wooden stand provided with the Gallery Glass® Frame Blank or display on a small easel. Optional: Stain or paint stand to match your decor, if desired. Place a votive candle behind the candle window stand.

Using the Direct Technique

1 Work on a flat surface protected with newspaper. Place the design blank directly over desired pattern in book.

2 Remove simulated leading top and seal, then replace the top. Remove the small cap from the simulated leading bottle. Using a nutpick or toothpick, make a hole in the tip. Be certain the hole is large enough; small holes will not allow the leading to flow freely. Replace the cap. Hold the bottle upside down and tap firmly on a hard surface to force the leading into the tip. Remove small cap.

3 Hold the bottle upside down and tap firmly on a hard surface to force the leading into the tip.

4 Hold the inverted bottle like a broom handle. Do not rest your elbow on your work surface—it will inhibit your movement. Squeeze the bottle. As the leading begins to flow, touch it to a pattern line. Apply even pressure and a uniform cord of simulated leading will form. Keep the bottle tip one inch above the work surface. Let the leading drape onto the pattern line by moving your arm smoothly and steadily. When you are near the end of a pattern line, stop squeezing.

5 Work from the inside to the outside until all pattern lines have been leaded, turning the design as needed.

6 Remove design blank from book. Let leading dry for at least 8 hours on a dry, flat surface with good air circulation, such as the top of the refrigerator, before painting. Do not dry in an oven or microwave.

7 Remove leading errors with a razor blade or craft knife to score unwanted sections, peel off and reapply.

8 Begin painting glass paint into pattern areas. Work one color of paint at a time, working from the inside to the outside of the pattern, turning the design as needed. First apply paint around the perimeter of the leading, then fill in the center. Add a generous amount of color, almost as high as the leading. NOTE: The glass paint is milky when applied, but will be clear when dry.

9 With a toothpick or nutpick, stroke back and forth quickly in straight lines through the paint, smoothing the grain. All colors should be combed. Crystal Clear can be left un-combed to create a bumpy effect, or it can be applied with a brush. Do not over-comb. Clean toothpick between colors. After applying paint to a few sections, pick up the project and use the toothpick to firmly tap under each painted section to remove bubbles.

10 Check paint coverage periodically. If there are streaks or light areas, you are using too little paint. Uniformly fill each section, work up to the leading lines, comb and tap.

11 Let glass paint dry at least 8 hours and cure at least 72 hours. Drying time may vary due to humidity, temperature, and thickness of application.

12 Let project cure at least one week before cleaning. To clean, spray a light mist of water on a soft cloth. Wipe the surface gently with the cloth to remove dust.

Ivy Privacy Desk Screen

Pictured on page 117.

GATHER THESE SUPPLIES

2 oz. Glass Paint:
03 = Cameo Ivory
08 = Kelly Green
11 = Blue Diamond

Other Supplies:
Hot glue gun and glue sticks

INSTRUCTIONS

Prepare:
1. See "Patterns" on page 115. Place the precut leading blank directly over patterns on pages 118-119.

Apply:
2. See "How to Create Glass Art Designs" on pages 115-117. Apply simulated leading and paint.

3. Apply hot glue to the grooves on the center screen, using a hot glue gun and hot glue. While the glue is hot, attach the sides to the center screen.

Pattern Actual Size

Pattern Actual Size   Use this pattern for both side panels of the screen.

Magnolia Candle Window

Pictured on page 120.

GATHER THESE SUPPLIES

2 oz. Glass Paint:
01 = Crystal Clear
02 = Snow White
03 = Cameo Ivory
20 = Amber
24 = Ivy Green

Other Supplies
Small easel
Tea light candle

Prepare:
1. See "Patterns" on page 115. Place the precut leading blank directly over pattern on page 121 in the book .

Apply:
2. See "How to Create Glass Art Designs" on pages 115-117. Apply simulated leading and paint.

3. Place your painted window in small easel.

Hummingbird Candle Window

Pictured on page 120.

GATHER THESE SUPPLIES

2 oz. Glass Paint:
01 = Crystal Clear
02 = Snow White
03 = Cameo Ivory
07 = Cocoa Brown
08 = Kelly Green
09 = Emerald Green
15 = Ruby Red
17 = Magenta Royal

Continued on page 120.

Continued from page 119.

Other Supplies
Small easel
Tea light candle

INSTRUCTIONS

Prepare:
1. See "Patterns" on page 115.
Place the precut leading blank
directly over pattern on page
122 in the book.

Apply:
2. See "How to Create Glass
Art Designs" on pages 115-
117. Apply simulated leading
and paint.

3. Place your painted window
in small easel.

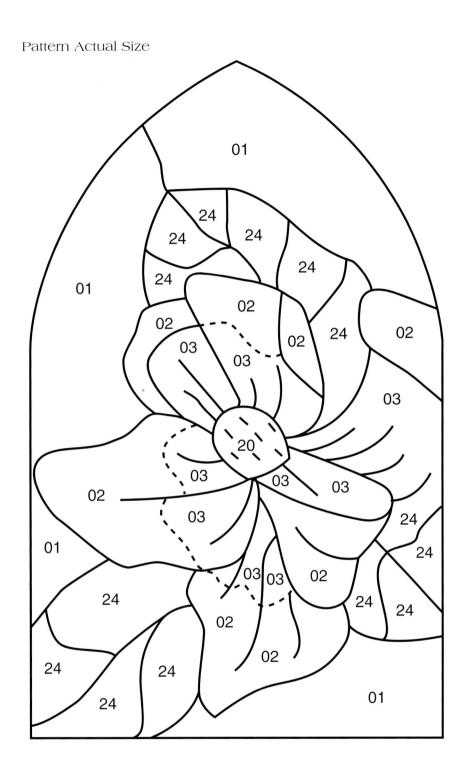

Birdhouse Candle Window

Pictured on page 120.

GATHER THESE SUPPLIES

2 oz. Glass Paint:
01 = Crystal Clear
04 = Sunny Yellow
05 = Orange Poppy
09 = Emerald Green
23 = Berry Red
24 = Ivy Green

Other Supplies:
Small easel
Tea light candle

INSTRUCTIONS

Prepare:
1. See "Patterns" on page 115. Place the precut leading blank directly over pattern on page 122 in the book.

Apply:
2. See "How to Create Glass Art Designs" on pages 115-117. Apply simulated leading and paint.

3. Place your painted window in small easel.

Pattern Actual Size

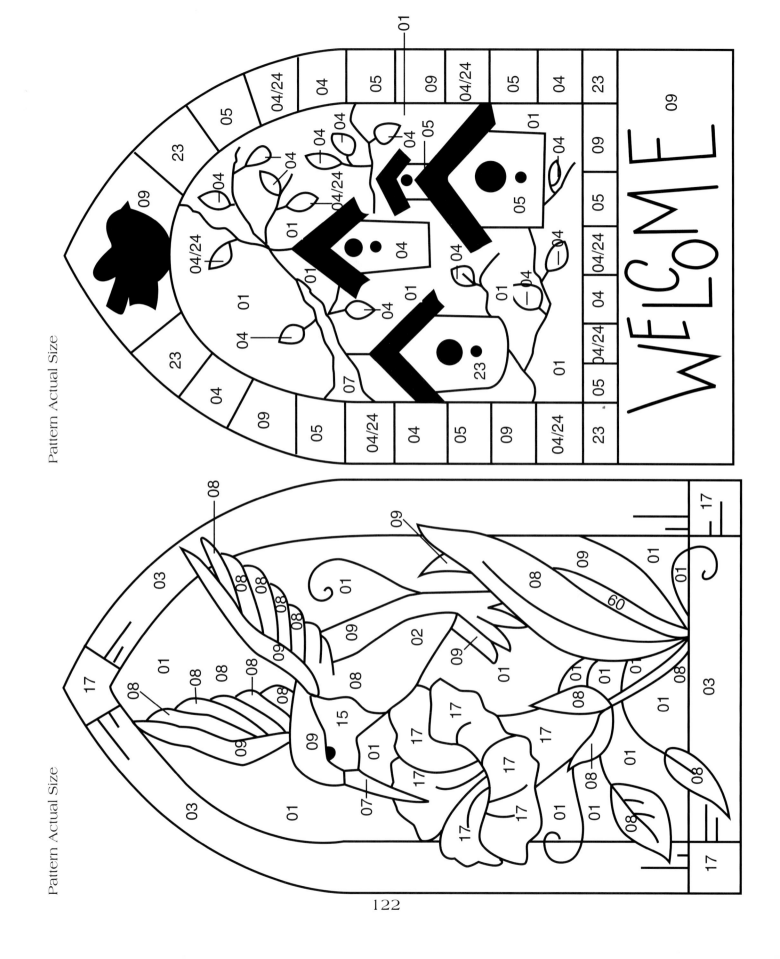

Pattern Actual Size

Pansy Frame

It is so easy and so personal to create glass art frames. You can make the window opening any size to fit your photo, then paint a sparkling design around it. Here, a garden fresh pansy enhances this photo from the backside of your painted glass art frame.

GATHER THESE SUPPLIES

2 oz. Glass Paint:
04 = Sunny Yellow
09 = Emerald Green
14 = Amethyst
21 = White Pearl

Other Supplies:
Desired photo
Small easel
Transparent tape

INSTRUCTIONS

Prepare:
1. See "Patterns" on page 115. Place the precut leading blank directly over pattern on page 124 in the book.

Apply:
2. See "How to Create Glass Art Designs" on pages 115-117. Apply simulated leading and paint.

3. Tape photo to back of painted frame. Place your painted frame in the small easel.

Sun & Moon Frame

The design on the child's photo frame lets everyone know that her parents would give her the sun and the moon, if they could.

GATHER THESE SUPPLIES

2 oz. Glass Paint:
02 = Snow White
12 = Royal Blue
20 = Amber

Other Supplies:
Desired photo
Small easel
Transparent tape

INSTRUCTIONS

Prepare:
1. See "Patterns" on page 115. Place the precut leading blank directly over pattern on page 124 in the book.

Apply:
2. See "How to Create Glass Art Designs" on pages 115-117. Apply simulated leading and paint.

3. Tape photo to back of painted frame. Place your painted frame in the small easel.

Product Sources

Plaid Enterprises, Inc., distributes Gallery Glass® Products that are used to create the projects throughout this book. Following is a listing of the product numbers for the various Gallery Glass products that are available.

Gallery Glass® Window Color™:
Translucent textured glass art paint that creates the look of authentic stained glass. This product is available in 2 oz. bottles in the following colors:

#16001 Crystal Clear (8 oz.)

#16002 Snow White

#16003 Cameo Ivory

#16004 Sunny Yellow

#16005 Orange Poppy

#16006 Canyon Coral

#16007 Cocoa Brown

#16008 Kelly Green

#16009 Emerald Green

#16010 Denim Blue

#16011 Blue Diamond

#16012 Royal Blue

#16013 Slate Blue

#16014 Amethyst

#16015 Ruby Red

#16016 Rose Quartz

#16017 Magenta Royal

#16018 Charcoal Black

#16019 Gold Sparkle

#16020 Amber

#16021 White Pearl

#16022 Clear Frost

#16023 Berry Red

#16024 Ivy Green

Gallery Glass® Simulated Liquid Leading:

#16025 2 oz. size

#16082 8 oz. size

Gallery Glass® Leading Blanks:
Blank sheets of material on which to make liquid lead lines.

#16051 Leading Blank

Gallery Glass® Styrene Blanks:
Blanks can be painted then frame, suspended, or cut into shapes.

#16052 Styrene Blank

Gallery Glass Precut Blank Shapes:
Precut blank shapes can place directly on pattern to be leaded and painted.

#16209 3-Panel Screen

#16211 Frame

#16212 Candle Window

Tip-Pen™ Craft Tips Set:
Tips dispense paints, glues, and a variety of mediums exactly where you want and in the quantity you choose.

#2527 Tip-Pen Craft Tips Set

Metric Conversion Chart

INCHES TO MILLIMETRES AND CENTIMETRES

INCHES	MM	CM	INCHES	CM	INCHES	CM
⅛	3	0.3	9	22.9	30	76.2
¼	6	0.6	10	25.4	31	78.7
½	13	1.3	12	30.5	33	83.8
⅝	16	1.6	13	33.0	34	86.4
¾	19	1.9	14	35.6	35	88.9
⅞	22	2.2	15	38.1	36	91.4
1	25	2.5	16	40.6	37	94.0
1¼	32	3.2	17	43.2	38	96.5
1½	38	3.8	18	45.7	39	99.1
1¾	44	4.4	19	48.3	40	101.6
2	51	5.1	20	50.8	41	104.1
2½	64	6.4	21	53.3	42	106.7
3	76	7.6	22	55.9	43	109.2
3½	89	8.9	23	58.4	44	111.8
4	102	10.2	24	61.0	45	114.3
4½	114	11.4	25	63.5	46	116.8
5	127	12.7	26	66.0	47	119.4
6	152	15.2	27	68.6	48	121.9
7	178	17.8	28	71.1	49	124.5
8	203	20.3	29	73.7	50	127.0

YARDS TO METRES

YARDS	METRES	YARDS	METRES	YARDS	METRES	YARDS	METRES	YARDS	METRES
⅛	0.11	2⅛	1.94	4⅛	3.77	6⅛	5.60	8⅛	7.43
¼	0.23	2¼	2.06	4¼	3.89	6¼	5.72	8¼	7.54
⅜	0.34	2⅜	2.17	4⅜	4.00	6⅜	5.83	8⅜	7.66
½	0.46	2½	2.29	4½	4.11	6½	5.94	8½	7.77
⅝	0.57	2⅝	2.40	4⅝	4.23	6⅝	6.06	8⅝	7.89
¾	0.69	2¾	2.51	4¾	4.34	6¾	6.17	8¾	8.00
⅞	0.80	2⅞	2.63	4⅞	4.46	6⅞	6.29	8⅞	8.12
1	0.91	3	2.74	5	4.57	7	6.40	9	8.23
1⅛	1.03	3⅛	2.86	5⅛	4.69	7⅛	6.52	9⅛	8.34
1¼	1.14	3¼	2.97	5¼	4.80	7¼	6.63	9¼	8.46
1⅜	1.26	3⅜	3.09	5⅜	4.91	7⅜	6.74	9⅜	8.57
1½	1.37	3½	3.20	5½	5.03	7½	6.86	9½	8.69
1⅝	1.49	3⅝	3.31	5⅝	5.14	7⅝	6.97	9⅝	8.80
1¾	1.60	3¾	3.43	5¾	5.26	7¾	7.09	9¾	8.92
1⅞	1.71	3⅞	3.54	5⅞	5.37	7⅞	7.20	9⅞	9.03
2	1.83	4	3.66	6	5.49	8	7.32	10	9.14

Index